THOMAS MORE

☞ Books in the RENAISSANCE LIVES series explore and illustrate the life histories and achievements of significant artists, rulers, intellectuals and scientists in the early modern world. They delve into literature, philosophy, the history of art, science and natural history and cover narratives of exploration, statecraft and technology.

Series Editor: François Quiviger

Already published

Albrecht Dürer: Art and Autobiography *David Ekserdjian*
Aldus Manutius: The Invention of the Publisher *Oren Margolis*
Andreas Vesalius: Anatomy and the World of Books *Sashiko Kusukawa*
Annibale Carracci: Art, Wit and Authority *F. M. Gage*
Artemisia Gentileschi and Feminism in Early Modern Europe *Mary D. Garrard*
Benvenuto Cellini and the Embodiment of the Modern Artist *Andreas Beyer*
Bernard Palissy and the Arts of the Earth *François Quiviger*
Blaise Pascal: Miracles and Reason *Mary Ann Caws*
Botticelli: Artist and Designer *Ana Debenedetti*
Caravaggio and the Creation of Modernity *Troy Thomas*
Descartes: The Renewal of Philosophy *Steven Nadler*
Domenico Ghirlandaio: An Elite Artisan and His World *Jean K. Cadogan*
Donatello and the Dawn of Renaissance Art *A. Victor Coonin*
Erasmus of Rotterdam: The Spirit of a Scholar *William Barker*
Filippino Lippi: An Abundance of Invention *Jonathan K. Nelson*
Francis I: The Knight-King *Glenn Richardson*
Francisco de Zurbarán and the Fabric of the World *Jeremy Robbins*
Giorgione's Ambiguity *Tom Nichols*
Hans Holbein: The Artist in a Changing World *Jeanne Nuechterlein*
Hans Memling and the Merchants *Mitzi Kirkland-Ives*
Hieronymus Bosch: Visions and Nightmares *Nils Büttner*
Impossible Nature: The World of Giuseppe Arcimboldo *Jessica Keating*
Isaac Newton and Natural Philosophy *Niccolò Guicciardini*
Jan van Eyck within His Art *Alfred Acres*
John Donne: In the Shadow of Religion *Andrew Hadfield*
John Evelyn: A Life of Domesticity *John Dixon Hunt*
Leon Battista Alberti: The Chameleon's Eye *Caspar Pearson*
Leonardo da Vinci: Self, Art and Nature *François Quiviger*
Lorenzo Ghiberti: Designer *Scott Nethersole*
Lucas Cranach: From German Myth to Reformation *Jennifer Nelson*
Machiavelli: From Radical to Reactionary *Robert Black*
Michelangelo and the Viewer in His Time *Bernadine Barnes*
Paolo Veronese and the Nobility of Painting *Tom Nichols*
Paracelsus: An Alchemical Life *Bruce T. Moran*
Petrarch: Everywhere a Wanderer *Christopher S. Celenza*
Piero della Francesca and the Invention of the Artist *Machtelt Brüggen Israëls*
Piero di Cosimo: Eccentricity and Delight *Sarah Blake McHam*
Pieter Bruegel and the Idea of Human Nature *Elizabeth Alice Honig*
Raphael and the Antique *Claudia La Malfa*
Rembrandt's Holland *Larry Silver*
Robert Hooke's Experimental Philosophy *Felicity Henderson*
Rubens's Spirit: From Ingenuity to Genius *Alexander Marr*
Rudolf II: The Life and Legend of the Mad Emperor *Thomas DaCosta Kaufmann*
Salvator Rosa: Paint and Performance *Helen Langdon*
Thomas More: Humanism and Heresy *Andrew Hadfield and Joanne Paul*
Thomas Nashe and Late Elizabethan Writing *Andrew Hadfield*
Titian's Touch: Art, Magic and Philosophy *Maria H. Loh*
Tycho Brahe and the Measure of the Heavens *John Robert Christianson*
Ulisse Aldrovandi: Naturalist and Collector *Peter Mason*

THOMAS MORE

Humanism and Heresy

ANDREW HADFIELD
AND JOANNE PAUL

REAKTION BOOKS

For Quentin Skinner and in memory of Peter Mack

Published by Reaktion Books Ltd
2–4 Sebastian Street
London EC1V 0HE, UK
www.reaktionbooks.co.uk

First published 2026

EU GPSR Authorised Representative
Logos Europe, 9 rue Nicolas Poussin, 17000, La Rochelle, France
email: contact@logoseurope.eu

Printed and bound in India by Replika Press Pvt. Ltd

A catalogue record for this book is available from the British Library

ISBN 978 1 83639 252 1

COVER: Detail of Hans Holbein the Younger, *Thomas More*, 1527, oil on oak. The Frick Collection, New York, photo akg-images.

CONTENTS

NOTE ON THE TEXT

English-language quotations have been modernized for the ease of the reader (although some archaic words have been preserved when necessary to preserve the sense). Latin titles have been translated into English. Unless specified, all translations are from the modern translation used. The year is presumed to begin on 1 January (rather than 25 March). European names have not been Anglicized, except in direct quotations. Bible quotations are translations from the Vulgate.

Introduction

The question of identifying the 'real' Thomas More has plagued scholars and biographers for five hundred years. There are many overlapping layers to sift through, and significant gaps to contend with. Thomas More was a Renaissance humanist, a scholar who advocated for the study of ancient Greek and Roman texts and used them as a model for his own works. As has long been established, such humanists, writing at the dawn of the age of print, engaged in a form of self-presentation in their works that modern scholars have labelled 'self-fashioning'. More also participated in the exchange of religious 'polemics' – harshly critical texts – as part of the religious schism and conflict that has become known as the Reformation. In these, too, More took on literary personae and engaged in a form of self-fashioning to make his arguments more persuasive. Most frustrating to the modern scholar, perhaps, is that these two groupings of texts – the humanist and the religious polemic – seem to contain contradictions, resulting in what has been called the 'multiple Mores thesis': the idea that distinct 'Mores' can be identified and treated, due to this opposition present in his works, as well as what we know about his life. The irony-loving Thomas More might have appreciated the paradox in which we find ourselves: we are drowning in written sources – millions of words More produced in his own lifetime – and yet they only have the effect of obscuring their author even further.

Abandoning this search and focusing on his works in their contexts provides a welcome respite and yields helpful insights, which is what we concentrate on in this short book. More's combative Reformation polemics had precedent in his contributions to the debates between Renaissance humanism and medieval scholasticism, which More held to be overly academic, isolationist and elitist. There are a few central beliefs to which we can see More returning throughout his works, even if there are changes in emphasis aligned with the tumults of his time. These include the rejection of pride: a competitive individualistic impulse, which More saw as threatening cohesion of the communities of which he was a part. In similar ways, More decried the questioning of collective authority, expressed in representative institutions, for the plural and fragmented authority of 'anyone whatsoever'. Finally, More returned repeatedly to the remembrance of death as a way of combating individual pridefulness and reminding his readers of the artificiality of those things which divide us (money, social standing) and our natural, fundamental equality.

There are some choices and actions More took in his life which are consistent with these central beliefs, and there are some that are not. Many have and will admire More's loyalty, dedication and dutifulness, while others condemn his treatment of religious dissenters, his apparent duplicity and his stubbornness. Centuries of mythologizing and fictionalizing have invested these two versions of More with life and legacy.

This is neither a biography of Thomas More, though a short biography for context will follow, nor in any way an attempt to uncover the 'real' version of him. This is an exploration of his written outputs in their political, religious and literary contexts. The 'unreal', literary versions of More are just as fascinating and helpful to the reader to understand as any constructed 'real' More. And here we encounter another irony of which More would be appreciative. For we are faced with the realization that any 'real' More we attempt to patch together must, at the end of the day, be no more than an approximation of the truth of this complex and conflicted man. Therefore, as with virtually all Renaissance lives, we have to cite works and texts alongside each other rather than being able to rely on life writing and biographical facts to explain the 'literary' works.[1] The 'fictional' and the 'real' cannot be easily separated, however much we might want to prise them apart.

Rather than a biography, this book is what might be termed a 'critical life study', which surveys and analyses the life, work and achievements of Thomas More.[2] We read his works as evidence of his life and beliefs, where this is appropriate – a complicated and ambiguous task, as the works do not always tell us the truth about More's life even when they refer to him, and especially when they provide a fictionalized version of his life and thought, as in *Utopia*. In other places the works are read as works of literature, polemic, theology, history, and other subjects and genres, as is appropriate. We hope readers will find these distinctions and principles useful when they use the book.

Like many significant statesmen of the Tudor court, Thomas More emerged from a relatively obscure background. His family, he later wrote, was 'not famous, but honourable'.[3] More was born in London on 7 February 1478 to John and Agnes (née Graunger) More; their second child and eldest son, he was born after their wedding in 1474.[4] His father, John, was a lawyer in his late twenties who had been admitted to the legal community of Lincoln's Inn around the time of his marriage. This was already evidence of impressive social mobility, as John's own father – William More – had been a baker, who had died when John was just sixteen.[5] This mobility may have come via John's mother, Johanna (née Joye), whose father had been Master of the Fraternity of St Nicholas and a member of the Common Council of London. Thomas More's own mother, Agnes, also had important city connections.

LONDINVM F
GLIAE RE
Hæc est regia illa totius Angliæ ciuitas LONDINVM, ad flu-
uium Thamesim sita. Cæsari, vt plures existimat, Trinobantum
nuncupata, multarum gentium comertio nobilitata, exculta domib. ornata te-
plis, excelsa arcibus, claris ingenijs, viris omnium artium doctrinarumq. gene-
re præstantibus, percelebris. Deniq. omnium rerum copia, atque opum excelletia
mirabilis. Inuehit in eam totius orbis opes ipse Thamasis, onerarijs nauibus per
sexaginta millia passuum, ad vrbem præalto alueo nauigabilis.
The Cort
The Temple
Lamberth

Map of London, from Georg Braun and Franz Hogenberg, *Civitates orbis terrarium*, vol. 1 (1572).

Her father, Thomas Graunger, was a tallow chandler of some standing who was also a member of the Fraternity of St Nicholas.

More was five in 1483 when King Edward IV died. The king's heir was his young son, Edward V, whose crown was quickly usurped by Richard, Duke of Gloucester, who became Richard III. These events had a profound effect on the young More, who later wrote about them in his unfinished work, *The History of King Richard III*. He drew on witness accounts and his father's testimony, as well as his own recollections of some of the more public events that took place in London that summer.

More's formal education probably began two years later, around the time of Henry VII's conquest and accession. He was enrolled at the only free grammar school in London at the time, St Anthony's Threadneedle Street, a school associated with the hospital of the same name and St Benet Fink Church. There he learned the fundamentals of Latin grammar, though he later criticized the outdated rote methods used. 'In the study of grammar,' he wrote, 'it should be enough to learn those empirical precepts which prepare you to speak Latin yourself and to read it intelligently, but not anxiously to seek out innumerable rules of speech or to squander your life over letters and syllables.'[6] He also criticized the handbooks used, which required a knowledge of Latin to teach the learning of Latin.

It was almost certainly through his father's connections that Thomas More was placed, around the age of twelve, in the household of the Archbishop of Canterbury and Lord Chancellor, John Morton, at Lambeth Palace.[7] More's son-in-law, William Roper, later reported that More had the honour of serving at Morton's table and was even involved in some of the dramatic productions performed at Lambeth, perhaps those by Henry Medwall, who was also resident at Lambeth at the time. Certainly, More continued his education while in Morton's service, and would later praise the innovative techniques of another Latin master at

Lambeth, John Holt – who became a close friend – who wrote his Latin instruction for schoolboys in English.[8]

After approximately two years at Lambeth, More began his studies at the University of Oxford around the age of fourteen. This was a common-enough age to begin a degree in the sixteenth century, though there were efforts to raise the age of entry to sixteen. For the most part, these had failed. Just a few years before More's arrival, an adolescent named Thomas Wolsey had graduated the four-year programme at the age of only fifteen. He was known, because of this accomplishment, as the 'boy bachelor'.

There is some debate around which college More studied at while at Oxford, but most biographers have settled on Canterbury College, given Morton's connections there. This college was largely inhabited by Benedictine monks, about ninety by the middle of the fifteenth century, though there were also 'sojourners', who were not required to take monastic vows to study there, alongside *pueri collegii* (boys of the college) on scholarships, three of whom were chosen by the archbishop himself.[9] It seems likely, given More's upbringing, that he was one of these *pueri*.

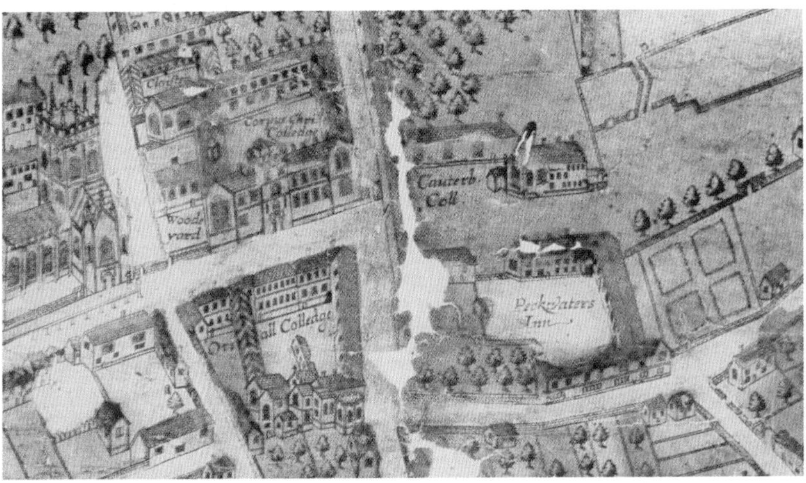

Buildings of Canterbury College, detail from Ralph Agas's plan of Oxford, *c*. 1578–88.

At Oxford, More received a fairly traditional scholastic education, though punctuated with influences from a new scholarly movement, the *studia humanitatis* (the study of humanity), which had been transmitted from the continent. Its proponents critiqued the medieval curriculum, with its focus on logic and abstraction,

Hans Holbein the Younger, *Sir John More*, *c.* 1526–7, coloured chalks on paper.

vehemently decrying the ignorance of the 'theologians' or 'scholastics' to real-world concerns. It was the same argument that More, influenced by their views, would later make regarding the study of grammar; these obscure and abstract rules were imposed by men with no reference to and impact on the real world. Students at Oxford, More later reflected, 'must also learn prudence in human affairs'.[10] By the time More arrived, a number of humanist reformers had already established themselves at Oxford. Of the older generation was William Celling, who as a young man had been a Benedictine monk at Canterbury College before travelling in Europe, bringing some of the new Renaissance learning with him.[11] About a decade before More was at Oxford, Celling had made a significant donation of books to his former college. Celling's student Thomas Linacre, a fellow of All Souls College who may previously have been a *puer* at Canterbury, had accompanied his master to Italy and remained there until his return to London in 1499.[12] Contemporary at Oxford with More was William Grocyn, who returned from his three-year trip to the continent in 1491 to give the first Greek public lectures at the university. More later credited Oxford for 'whatever learning I do have' and for giving him the 'rudiments' to pursue greater and deeper study.[13]

More did not finish his degree at Oxford, returning to London after just two years. This was a common path, especially for lawyers with civic ambitions. Later, it was claimed that More had been dragged away from Oxford by his father, who had strong-armed the boy away from his books and back into the bustling world of the city.[14] John More's own career had progressed from strength to strength, including twice holding the position of Governor of Lincoln's Inn, his second time in the role concurrent with the year that his son returned to London.

Thomas More did not immediately become a member of Lincoln's Inn, or indeed any of the Inns of Court, but instead at one of the Inns of Chancery, New Inn, a preparatory institution for young aspiring lawyers, who would then move on to one of the Inns of Court.[15] The purpose of More's instruction was to develop an intimate knowledge of the common law and, despite its differing content, in its delivery it was an education that differed little from the type of instruction that More had encountered at Oxford.[16] Essential to More and his peers' learning was the 'putting of cases', in which an imaginary case would be 'mooted' to stimulate debate and simulate bringing a case to the courts. Many involved a conversational back-and-forth, with the case becoming increasingly complex with each new addition of speculative circumstance.

In the spare moments he could find, Thomas More continued the classical studies he had pursued at Oxford. These pursuits put him in the company of other English intellectuals whose scholarly accomplishments were helping them rise above their humble backgrounds and gain renown and position in the city, country and beyond. There were four men, in particular, with whom More made up an academic coterie, and with whom he became well acquainted following his admission to Lincoln's Inn. Together they formed one of the most intellectually powerful coterie groups in Europe. All were university educated, and all had spent time studying with the masters on the continent, primarily in Italy. The eldest, William Grocyn, was perhaps as much as thirty years older than More and was likely familiar to More from his time at Oxford. In 1496 he took up the position of vicar at St Lawrence Jewry, near Cheapside. More referred to Grocyn as 'the sole guide of my life', at least in the absence of another member of the group, John Colet.[17] Colet had returned from a trip to Rome about the time More became a member of Lincoln's Inn and settled into a teaching position at Oxford. William Lily, Grocyn's godson, whom More referred to as 'the dearest partner of my endeavours', had just returned from Italy himself. The last was Thomas Linacre, 'my master in learning' as More referred to him, who was also about two decades older than the young More. Linacre returned from Italy by August 1499 and was appointed tutor to none other than the heir to the throne, Prince Arthur.

More himself had the opportunity to enter such esteemed royal circles in the summer of 1499. Having spent three years at Lincoln's Inn (he was admitted on 12 February 1496), More was invited to the Greenwich home of William Blount, Baron Mountjoy. Mountjoy had spent the previous year in Paris, where he was tutored by the Dutch scholar Erasmus, whom he had invited back to England with him. Alongside More's friend, Edward Arnold, from Lincoln's Inn, More and Erasmus journeyed to the nearby Eltham Palace, where they were greeted by the second-in-line to the throne, the eight-year-old Prince Henry, along with his two sisters, Margaret and Mary, and infant brother, Edmund. More impressed the prince with a gift of writing, which irked Erasmus, who had not been sufficiently prepared. Nevertheless, by the end of the year, the two scholars were corresponding.

Central to their intellectual friendship was the study of Greek, which More took up in earnest at the turn of the century, with Grocyn as his teacher. It was almost certainly Grocyn who also arranged More's lectures at St Lawrence Jewry on the topic of *The City of God* by St Augustine. More's lectures, according to Erasmus, drew 'large audiences', and 'priests and old men were not ashamed to seek instruction in holy things from a young man and a layman, or sorry they had done so.'[18]

St Lawrence Jewry was also a hub for the powerful and wealthy Mercers' Company.[19] Grocyn, as its vicar, was closely tied up with the mercers and frequently the recipient of their final bequests. Another of More's humanist friends, Colet, was the son of a high-ranking mercer who had served as mayor of London for two terms. More's own father, John, had solidified his ties with the mercers shortly after the death of Thomas's mother in 1499. Within a year of his first wife's death, he married the rich and

eminently capable Joan Fyler Marchall, the daughter and (twice) widow of mercers.[20] John More would go on to marry a further two mercer widows in the coming decades.

The first pieces of More's writing that can be dated come from this period. The first is a letter from More to John Holt,

Hans Holbein the Younger, *The Dance of Death: The Empress*, c. 1526, woodcut.

the former Latin master of Lambeth, in which (among other things) More describes the entry of Catherine of Aragon into the city, before her wedding to Henry VII's heir, Prince Arthur. More was fulsome in his praise of the Spanish princess, though disparaging of her Spanish escort, particularly those he described as 'Ethiopians'.[21] The second is a reflection on a more sombre royal occasion, the death of Catherine's new mother-in-law, Queen Elizabeth of York. 'Ye that put your trust & confidence,/ In worldly riches & frail prosperity,' he had the dead queen proclaim, 'Remember death & look here upon me.'[22] The poem is a reflection on the importance of the remembrance of death, a figure who strips mortals of all worldly wealth and distinction, a theme that recurs in More's writing.

It was also at this time that More took up residence in the vicinity of the London Charterhouse. Whether or not More, as Erasmus later reported, spent the time grappling with the possibility of taking Holy Orders himself, by 1504 he had certainly made a decision, marrying Jane Colt, the young daughter of an Essex gentleman. More's friend Erasmus would later reflect that More chose for his wife 'an unmarried girl who was still very young . . . which gave him the more opportunity to mould her character to match his own'.[23] More himself, in his reflections on 'how to choose a wife', suggested that the reader select a wife who is 'just finishing her education or ready to begin it immediately' – Jane was probably in the former category – for 'if she is well instructed herself, then someday she will teach your little grandsons, at an early age, to read.'[24] Jane gave birth to at least four children between 1505 and 1509 – Margaret, Elizabeth, Cecily and John – while the family was resident at a home known as The Barge, on Bucklersbury, leased from the Mercers' Company.[25] It was there that, in March 1505, Erasmus came to stay, and the two scholars translated works by the controversial Greek prose writer and satirist Lucian of Samosata. Erasmus may have inspired

More to take his first visit to the continent, which he did in 1508, visiting the universities at Paris and Leuven, both of which had connections to the Dutch scholar.[26]

The year 1509 was a significant one for Thomas More. His only son was born and he was made a member of the Mercers'

Thomas More's 'Verses on the Coronation of Henry VIII', London, 1509.

Company, thus admitted to the freedom of London as a citizen.[27] A month later, King Henry VII died and was succeeded by his only surviving son, Henry VIII (Prince Arthur had died not long after his wedding to Catherine of Aragon). On his accession Henry VIII married his brother's widow, having secured a dispensation for consanguinity – or closeness of blood – from the pope, needed in order to marry a woman who was, in the eyes of the Church and the law, his sister. More composed a 'Coronation Ode' to celebrate the new king and queen and presented a copy to his sovereign. He and his scholarly friends welcomed the new regime, seeing Henry as one of their own for his humanist education and promises of support for scholars.

Perhaps tempted by the offers of employment that accompanied the new reign, Erasmus visited again not long after the coronation, once again taking up residence with the More family. While there he composed another work of praise, which he wittily entitled *Moriae encomium*, meaning both 'praise of Folly' – as it was, in content, a praise of the notion of Folly – but also 'praise of More'. The model for Folly's well-connected worldly scholar, More certainly lived up to his encomium, participating in his first major negotiations on behalf of the Mercers' Company, while Erasmus wrote away in his study at The Barge. European politics had put the trade relationship between the major cloth-selling city of Antwerp and the merchants of London at risk, and More was tasked with negotiating with Antwerp's representative. More did so with panache, and a few months later was elected to the House of Commons for Henry VIII's first parliament, replacing a mercer.[28] A month later, with Parliament closed, More also became one of the two undersheriffs of London, serving as judge of the Sheriff's Court for the Poultry Compter.[29] If this were not enough, More also continued his scholarship, producing a translation – with his own amendments – of the *Life of Pico Mirandola*.[30]

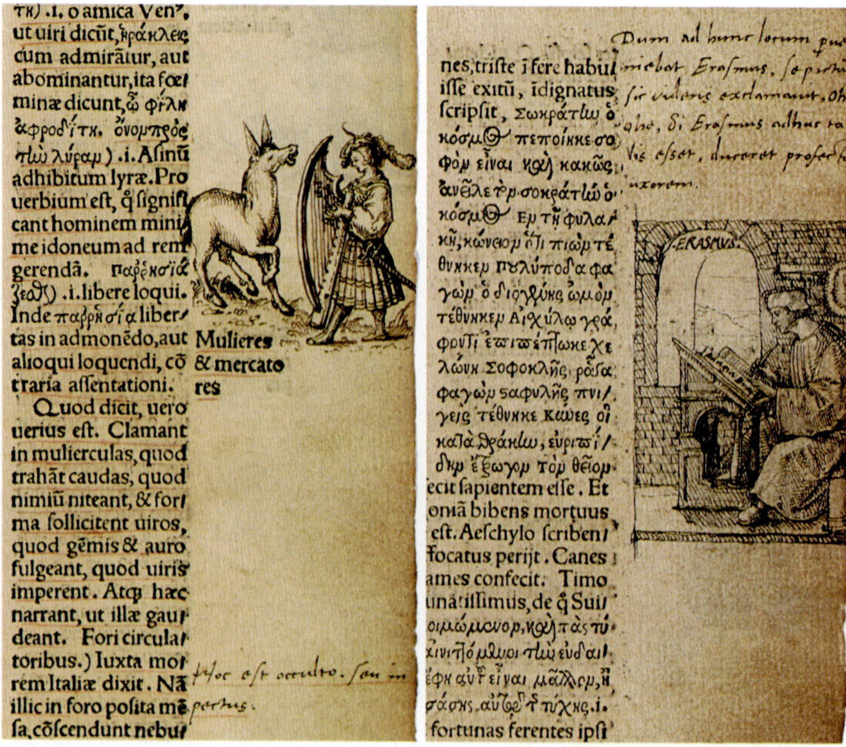

In 1511 More's wife, Jane, died. More – almost certainly overburdened by professional and scholarly commitments and with four children under the age of six – remarried with scandalous haste by means of a dispensation and small payment to the local rector. His wife was Alice (née Harpur) Middleton, another mercer widow, who added her eight-year-old daughter to The Barge.

With Alice running the household, More was able to spend more time at work. He began his *History of King Richard III* in about 1513, though it remained unfinished when he ceased working on it six years later. He was involved in supporting the war with France,

Marginal illustrations by Ambrosius Holbein and Hans Holbein the Younger in a 1515 copy of Erasmus of Rotterdam, *The Praise of Folly*, pen and ink.

Hans Holbein the Younger, *Lady Alice More*, *c.* 1530, oil on wood.

which had broken out in 1512, chosen as the representative of the city of London to the court regarding the French War.[31] He heard at first hand, from his brother-in-law, John Rastell, one of two hundred men serving under the Privy Councillor Sir Edward Belknap, the 'disasters' experienced during the campaign.[32] In the midst of the peace negotiations, More was also drawn into a high-profile case over the seizure of alum, a valuable substance used to tan leather, belonging to the pope.[33] More helped to negotiate a delicate settlement with the eyes of the king and his leading minister, Thomas Wolsey, on him.

More's successes with the Mercers' Company and in the case of the pope's alum are probably what secured his place on a trade mission to Flanders in the summer of 1515. When talks in Bruges stalled, and with few funds to sustain his stay in the city, More travelled to nearby Antwerp, visiting a friend of Erasmus's, Pieter Gillis. With a mind full of trade negotiations, warfare, competition and penury, More reflected on a traditional humanist question: what is the best state of the commonwealth? In other words, what would the ideal state look like, and how could it be established? The idea may have begun in simple discussions with Gillis, or perhaps a humanist game – not unlike the lawyer's 'putting of cases'. These ideas became Book Two of More's best-known work, *Utopia*.

Utopia, however, was not the only piece of writing he penned during this long summer on the continent. He also composed his 'Letter to Dorp'. Begun as a defence of Erasmus, following Maarten van Dorp's critique of *Praise of Folly*, the letter was also a defence of the entire enterprise of humanism, and More warned in it that should heretics adopt the prideful learning of the theologians, who think that 'they alone can interpret the writings of all men, and even sacred scripture itself, in whatever sense happens to suit them,' there will be no end to disputing.[34]

More at last returned to London at the end of October, months later than he had originally expected. Despite the delays, the mission had ultimately been successful, and it was for this reason that More reported to Erasmus that the king had offered him an annuity, one which he was determined to refuse, however, as it risked the trust of those with whom he worked in the city.[35] Over the course of 1516, he reflected on the pull of the court in Book One of his *Utopia*, which he added to the manuscript he had carried back with him from the continent. Struggling to finish the book in the busyness of his life back in London, he at last sent it off to Erasmus towards the end of 1516 and it was published in Leuven at the end of that year.

More's involvement in seeking to put a stop to the Evil May Day riot of 1517, and in its bloody aftermath, may have played a part in his eventual decision to abandon his role in the city and take up one in the court. More failed to talk down the rioters in the early hours of 1 May, but more importantly, as undersheriff, he was involved in the investigations as to the riot's causes as part of the massive wave of trials and executions that followed. Less than a year later, in March 1518, More was formally sworn into the king's service. He later claimed that this included the king's admonition that he 'first look unto God and after God, unto him.'[36] Around the same time, he received a letter from Erasmus which included a package of texts, which the Dutchman sent to his friend for comment. One was a small pamphlet, which Erasmus identified as 'Conclusions on Papal Pardons' but was properly titled *Disputatio pro declaratione virtutis indulgentiarum*: 'A disputation on the power of indulgences'.[37] It contained 95 theses critical of the Catholic Church, written by a lecturer at the University of Wittenberg, Martin Luther.

More was not pulled into the debate over Luther's attack on the Church for another several years, claiming too little time to engage with Luther's texts.[38] This was probably true. His service to the king primarily took the form of acting as an intermediary between the king and Cardinal Wolsey, giving More a role, for

instance, in the negotiations over the Treaty of London in 1518 and granting him an invitation to the Field of the Cloth of Gold celebrations in 1520.

England's condemnation of Luther came the following year, when in May 1521 Luther's books were publicly burned. More's friend John Fisher, Bishop of Rochester, preached over the flames, and Wolsey held up the king's own writings on the matter, the *Assertio septem sacramentorum* (Defence of the Seven Sacraments), for which Henry received the title of *Fidei Defensor* (Defender of the Faith) from the pope. More later claimed he had little to do with this text, aside from advising the king on a few points, including toning down arguments for the pope's supremacy, in case the two should ever come into conflict in the future.[39]

More was still producing works of his own, including a public letter to his former university and a reflection on the Christian *Four Last Things*: Death, Judgement, Heaven and Hell. This latter piece may have been written as an exercise shared with his eldest daughter, Margaret.[40] At almost sixteen, Margaret More was a highly trained and skilled humanist scholar. Her father had established something of a small school at Bucklersbury, which included his four children and the other young people of

British school, *The Field of the Cloth of Gold*, c. 1545, oil on canvas.

standing who joined his household, either passing through or on a more permanent basis. A central tenet of this little school was that the girls were educated alongside the boys.[41] Both women and men, he wrote to the children's tutor, 'are equally suited for the knowledge of learning by which reason is cultivated'.[42] He became an advocate for the education of women and girls, though the aim was to redress the natural defect and moral weakness in women, rather than prepare them for a public life. According to Erasmus, More's influence caused other noblemen and gentlemen to consider a similar track for their own daughters.[43]

Luther's rejoinder to Henry VIII appeared in late 1522, in which he called the English king 'damnable and offensive worm' and deserving to have his 'tongue and hands cut off' to prevent

Hans Holbein the Younger, *Margaret More Roper*, 1535–6, paint on vellum.

him ever speaking or writing again.[44] Henry could not answer Luther's attacks; he needed a man of lesser standing, but one of great scholarly ability, religious vehemence and patriotic zeal, and close enough to him to ensure that his response was aligned with Henry's own arguments. Thomas More was the natural choice. He produced two versions of his *Responsio ad Lutherum*, condemning Luther and his writings in the strongest terms.

As he revised the *Responsio*, he took up another role in the king's government, as Speaker of the House of Commons for the 1523 session of Parliament. According to Roper, More made a plea for what in modern terms would be called freedom of speech.[45] This assurance of the king's clemency in regard to 'boisterous and rude' advice was only meant for the House, however, and otherwise More maintained a fierce condemnation of those offering critique of the king. After all, even in Utopia, 'to take counsel on matters of common interest outside the senate or the popular assembly is considered a capital offense.'[46]

The next year, More and his growing family left The Barge and purchased lands and buildings in Chelsea.[47] In addition to his four children, the youngest of whom was fifteen, More had also taken in several wards, as well as his stepdaughter and her new husband, and welcomed a grandchild. The Barge was bursting at the seams and no longer fit for purpose. More's work no longer regularly took him to the Inns, Poultry or Guildhall, but to Westminster, Whitehall and the cardinal's new grand home at Hampton Court. Chelsea, to the west of the city along the Thames, was much more convenient and would give the family the room it needed.

At Chelsea, More also had more space to organize his books and papers and so spend more time writing. He penned his 'Letter to Bugenhagen' in 1526, reacting not only to the defence of Luther's principles by Johannes Bugenhagen but to what he had heard about recent events in Germany, including the German Peasants' War, the tragedy of which More laid at Luther's feet, viewing it

Henry VIII at the opening of Parliament, from the 'Wriothesley Garter Book', 1523, paint on vellum.

Hans Holbein the Younger, *Thomas More*, 1527, oil on oak.

as the logical consequence of a theology that disregarded the importance of works and crowned individual judgement over recognized authorities. More's harsh, panicked words were matched by action. In January 1526 More led a raid on the Steelyard in London, searching for prohibited Lutheran books. Four men were imprisoned and questioned before being publicly punished, carrying faggots before a crowd of hundreds.

In 1527 More was in his fiftieth year and had much to show for it. He displayed his standing and achievements proudly in two portraits he commissioned from Hans Holbein the Younger, recently arrived from the continent, and recommended to him by Erasmus. The first was a half-length of More, showing More dressed simply, but elegantly, his brown hair sticking out from the sides of his black cap, before a fringed green curtain, pulled loosely to More's right. Around More's neck hangs a golden collar, highlighting his service to the royal house, signified by the letter 'S', portcullises and a single Tudor rose.[48] More also wears red velvet sleeves, and an engraved gold ring with a central oval-cut stone. In his hand is a single folded piece of paper – perhaps waiting to be written upon, perhaps with a confidential message inside – a sign of his administrative responsibility and scholarly outputs.

The half-portrait was the less ambitious of the two projects Holbein completed for More. In addition to a further sketch of his patron, Holbein also drew studies of his father, wife and children. This was to produce a massive and unique family portrait on cloth, with no fewer than ten members of the household captured: his father, children, wards and the family fool, Henry Patenson, along with two secretaries.[49]

This calm familial scene captured at Chelsea was in stark contrast to the shocking news that came in from the continent in May 1527. The holy city of Rome, the home of the pope, had been sacked by troops fighting for Holy Roman Emperor Charles V, and the soldiers had committed unspeakable atrocities. More once again attributed the bloodshed to Lutheranism, as a large number of the ransacking soldiers had been German mercenaries.

The effects of the sacking of Rome on the European landscape were almost immediate. With Pope Clement VII taken prisoner by the emperor, the Defender of the Faith was motivated to finalize the treaty between England and France, and More was sent as part of the delegation led by Wolsey to reconfirm the terms. The cardinal, however, had another – secret – purpose while he, More and the rest of the company were in France. Henry VIII was seeking an annulment from his wife, Catherine of Aragon, after falling in love with one of her ladies, Anne Boleyn. Wolsey was to secure the support of the French for the annulment, which would undoubtedly be opposed by the emperor, Catherine's nephew. The real power who could grant Henry's wish was the pope, but after the sack of Rome, he remained the

Hans Holbein the Younger, *Study for the Family Portrait of Thomas More*, 1527, pen and brush over chalk drawing.

hostage of the emperor and was therefore unlikely to grant the English king's request.

Most of the senior men in the delegation were aware of this secret mission; it would have been hard for More not to have

Hans Holbein the Younger, *Anne Boleyn*, 1532–6, coloured chalks on paper.

known of it too. Nevertheless, it wasn't until his return in October 1527 that More was formally introduced to the 'King's Great Matter' by the king himself. Henry showed More the passage in Leviticus which prohibited marriage between a man and his brother's wife, and questioned whether the pope truly had the power to do away with such a clear scriptural injunction. It cannot have escaped More's notice that it was a similar question to the one that the Lutherans raised. More never publicly shared his response to the king, who asked him what he thought on the matter, though he noted that the king took what he said 'benignly' and suggested that More speak to others considering the matter, so it was unlikely to have been wholly in line with the king's wishes.[50]

In the new year, More was tasked with responding even more clearly – and in English – to the wealth of heretical texts that were entering the country, particularly those penned by the Englishman-in-exile William Tyndale. The result was the *Dialogue Concerning Heresy*, published in 1529. At the same time, a papal court was being convened to consider the matter of the king's marriage. Catherine had refused to go quietly, and maintained vociferously that she had not truly been married to Arthur for they had never consummated their relationship. The cardinal sent by the pope had been instructed to 'protract the matter as long as possible', which he did admirably.[51] When it was finally prorogued in July 1529, Henry had all but lost patience with both the foreign cardinal and his own. On the first day of the new legal term in October, Cardinal Thomas Wolsey was indicted for the crime of *praemunire*, appealing to papal power over and above the crown's authority.[52] Just over a week later, he formally handed over the Great Seal, the sign of his office as Lord Chancellor.

There was much debate as to whom the Seal and office would go to next. Wolsey had held the post of Lord Chancellor since 1515, as long as John Morton, longer than any other Chancellor for a hundred years. With very few, extremely short-lived exceptions, members of the clergy had held the position of Lord Chancellor for centuries. However, widespread anticlerical sentiment and Henry's own frustrations meant that the king and council were likely to be disinclined to appoint a leading churchman once again, who might prioritize loyalty to the pope over that to the king.

Several candidates were mooted, but in the end Thomas More was chosen as the next Lord Chancellor. He was in many ways an untraditional candidate but combined legal experience with theological knowledge and a deep understanding of politics. In criticizing Lutheranism he had shown himself fierce in his loyalty to the king, but equivocal on the authority of the pope. What's more, he had little power or authority outside of this role and might – some hoped – be easily controlled. They were soon disappointed. When asked again by the king for his view on the annulment, it became clear that the two men held different views, and More was promised that he would be excused from intervention 'in that matter'. Henry, More later reported, ended by reiterating what he had told him when he had first entered his service, twelve years before: 'that I should first look unto God and after God unto him'.[53]

Unfortunately, it soon became clear that much of the business of government was taken up with the King's 'great matter', and a refusal to engage with it was tantamount to self-imposed political exile. More agreed to sign the articles against Wolsey but refused to sign the letter to the pope, pressuring the pontiff on the king's need to divorce and remarry. Shockingly, More – the king's leading political official – had not been invited to attend the General Council that had produced the letter.[54]

There was one task, however, to which he could apply himself without 'ruffle or trouble of his conscience': the prosecution of heresy.[55] Technically, as Lord Chancellor More had no official role in the trial or sentencing of heretics, but it did make him 'Keeper of the King's Conscience', and thus the realm's. It was in his power to arrest suspected heretics, interrogate them and hand them to the religious courts for trial with the evidence he had collected.[56] Such men were imprisoned for anything from a few days up to several weeks in the gatehouse at Chelsea, where More kept a pair of stocks.[57] More used this time, he asserted, to try to turn them from their heresies, before they were convicted by the Church. He 'honestly entreated' and laboured for their 'amendment in as hearty loving manner' as he could.[58] His enemies said he tortured them.

He was fighting this battle on multiple fronts. He had not ceased his writing against heresy, though he had little time for it. The first part of his *Confutation of Tyndale's Answer* emerged during his time as Lord Chancellor. In this role, More was also overseeing the business of the House of Lords, which included a number of anticlerical policies. The king was especially keen to limit the power of Parliament's clerical parallel institution, Convocation. In early 1531 the king insisted that Convocation recognize him as 'sole protector and supreme head of the Anglican church and clergy'. The king's new rising minister, Thomas Cromwell, even entered the chamber where Convocation met to add his pressure to the discussions. In the end, under Archbishop of Canterbury William Warham's careful guidance, the king's supremacy was recognized, though with the added clause 'as far as the law of Christ allows'.[59] His compromise was met with silence from the assembled ecclesiastics. Warham laid before the hushed clerics an ancient legal assumption, *qui tacet consentire videtur* – 'he who is silent is taken to consent.'[60]

By Eastertide 1532 the anticlerical measures had reached a new height, summed up in a document presented to Convocation called the 'Submission of the Clergy', containing articles demanding almost unthinkable secular regulation of the spiritual.[61] When these did not pass immediately, the king moved swiftly, proroguing Parliament and ordering the prorogation of Convocation, once

Hans Holbein the Younger, *Thomas Cromwell*, 1532–3, oil on oak.

they had accepted the Submission of the Clergy. This they did, under the watchful eye of a delegation of lords who had come to impress the king's will upon them. The next day, More formally resigned his position of Lord Chancellor, handing the Great Seal to Henry VIII in the gardens at Whitehall Palace.

Following his resignation More had little else to occupy him than the drive to write. And write he did. Within months, he produced the second part of his *Confutation of Tyndale's Answer*, printed in 1533. It was the lengthiest and deepest refutation of Lutheranism that he had ever produced. That year also saw the publication of a further four books, all religious polemics: *The Apology of Thomas More*, *The Debellation of Salem and Bizance*, the *Letter Against Frith* and *Answer to a Poisoned Book*. From one perspective, More was simply continuing the work he had done for nearly a decade: opposing heretical texts with orthodoxy. The ground, however, had shifted beneath him. Henry VIII had appointed a new Lord Chancellor and an Archbishop of Canterbury (Warham had died in office) who were more amenable to his will and secured his divorce and remarriage to Anne Boleyn. The men More wrote against were no longer enemies of the regime; some were even employed by it.

And it was noticed. In January 1534 Cromwell's men raided the press of More's printer and nephew, William Rastell. Nothing incriminating was found, but it forced More to write to Cromwell, promising he would never produce anything countering the king's will. A few months later, More's name was included on an Act of Attainder against Elizabeth Barton, the Maid of Kent, a visionary whose prophecies and opposition to the king's divorce from Catherine of Aragon led to her death at Tyburn. He wrote with greater desperation to Cromwell, as well as the king, and in the end his name was dropped. Three days later, the Act of Succession was introduced, declaring that the daughter who had been born to Anne Boleyn the previous September, Elizabeth, was the heir to the throne, and not Henry VIII's daughter by

Catherine of Aragon, Mary, as this previous marriage was 'utterly void and annulled'. What's more, the preamble spoke of the illicit intervention of the 'Bishop of Rome' into the successions of Christian princes, establishing Henry as head of the Church, and denying the supremacy of the papacy. The act also set out that all subjects should be required to make an oath to 'observe, fulfil, maintain, defend, and keep' the contents of the act. Two weeks later, More was commanded to present himself at Lambeth Palace to take the oath. He refused and was imprisoned, first at Westminster Abbey and, finally, at the Tower of London.

More had left some writings unfinished when he departed Chelsea. These included a *Treatise on the Passion*, perhaps begun in those tense Lenten weeks between the introduction of the Act of Succession and More's arrest. He continued his rumination on these themes in the Tower, writing his *Dialogue of Comfort* and *De tristitia Christi*, as well as several elaborate letters, addressed to his daughter Margaret.

According to the Act of Succession, the penalty for refusal of the oath was forfeiture of goods and imprisonment, both of which More had already suffered. In November 1534, however, a new Treason Act was introduced to the Lords, setting out that the definition of treason was now expanded to include those who 'wish, will or desire by words of writing' any harm to the king, queen or heir 'or to deprive them of any of their dignity or title'. Treason was no longer just an act of bodily harm against the ruler and his family, but words that criticized or questioned them.[62]

A month after Easter 1535, the first treason trials under the new act were conducted. Five men – three Carthusian priors, a Brigittine monk and a secular priest – were sentenced to death for refusing the oath, and thus, it was reasoned, denying the king's title as Supreme Head of the Church. The day after their sentence was read out, More was once again asked to swear the oath, and once again he refused. Further examinations were carried out over the coming weeks against him and his servants, as well as against John Fisher, Bishop of Rochester, who had likewise refused to swear. Fisher was tried on 17 June and sentenced to death, an execution carried out on 22 June. Three days later the king issued a writ, declaring both Fisher and More to be traitors, a week before More's treason trial began on 1 July.

More was convicted on a charge of maliciously denying the king's supremacy, based on evidence presented by a fellow lawyer, Richard Rich, with whom More had engaged in a game of 'putting of cases' while Rich oversaw the removal of More's writing materials in the Tower. The jury returned a guilty verdict in only fifteen minutes and More's sentence was read out. According to Roper, More then finally publicly broke his silence on the matter, condemning the king's break with the Catholic Church.

He was executed on Tower Hill on 6 July. He had been asked to say only a few words, rather than give a lengthy scaffold speech, perhaps out of fear that he would repeat his performance at his trial. According to reports, his final words were, 'I die the king's good servant, and God's first.'

ONE

Early Humanist Writings

More is best known as a religious figure, but his career and writings were shaped by the *studia humanitatis* (the studies of humanity), and of his interest in humanism there can be little doubt.[1] Humanism was a response to the rediscovery of texts and manuscripts from the ancient world, principally Greece and Rome. It involved not only reading a new range of works that had been inaccessible to a European audience for centuries, but an educational system that moved away from the emphasis of the medieval school and university curriculum, which demanded the study of theology and logic, preparing students for a career in the Church. The significance of religion and formal philosophy continued, and until the seventeenth century a great proportion of students still entered the priesthood and related offices, but there was a new interest in the art of persuasion, rhetoric and the ability to speak and write well that was a result of reading and imitating the style of the ancient works known as the 'classics'. For some, good style, fine writing and extensive learning in stimulating old texts was quite enough.[2] For others, like More, humanism could be reconciled with Christianity, the works of the ancients pointing towards Christian revelation, providing a reinvigorating understanding of human history and enabling scholars to provide a more accurate understanding of scripture as the humanistic techniques of recovering and understanding secular texts were then applied to producing a better version of the Bible. Furthermore, the concentration on the study of man could lead to a nuanced and tolerant understanding of Christianity, one that emphasized human capacity to think, solve problems and so, its adherents believed, learn how to worship God more effectively than before.[3]

RELIGION AND TRUTH

The humanist-inspired developments to the education system also led to a much greater interest in political institutions and processes in Europe, from reading authors such as the Roman orator and lawyer Marcus Tullius Cicero (106–43 BCE), whose extensive writings outlined for later readers the complex functioning of public offices of the Roman Republic. Cicero's work became central to the curriculum in schools and universities and had a significant impact on More's thinking, especially in *Utopia*.[4] Humanist thinking led to an increased belief that learning could be applied to a public life of service in government. The curriculum encouraged students to think about how they might serve their country as well as the Church, and, as universities expanded, more graduates looked for careers in the institutions of state. More's career, balanced between Church and State, demonstrates how such new developments in thinking and education demanded sophisticated and complicated responses from those prepared to enter any form of active service.

More was largely taught in Latin at Oxford and he learned Greek from scholars such as William Grocyn and Thomas Linacre, and he then worked hard to become a skilful reader and writer of both languages, producing a range of writings in Latin, alongside those in English, before he entered the service of Henry VIII.[5] More seems to have been attracted to humanism for four main reasons. First, his career as a lawyer provided him with an obvious reason to be interested in rhetoric and the art of persuasion, vital tools for anyone working with the law (rhetoric having developed in tandem with the practice of the law, as its Latin proponents, such as Quintilian, recognized). More was probably most attracted to continuing his humanist studies after he graduated from Oxford, but he was persuaded, perhaps by his father, to pursue a legal career. Many observers, notably Erasmus, recognized a tension in More's loyalties and ambitions, between his life in public service and commitment to scholarship, a common dilemma for many who were inspired by humanism, and one openly discussed in *Utopia*.[6] Certainly, More was dedicated to his public life from an early age, working for the Mercers' Company, then acting as an undersheriff and finally taking the plunge to serve Henry VIII. More's humanist education qualified him for these roles, as well as providing him with a moral imperative for public service.

Second, More was always interested in establishing the truth – as a good lawyer should be – and methods of humanist enquiry sought to establish the most plausible explanation for any event, as well as the most likely origin. These were rigorous ways of thinking about the past, and ones we can see at work in his history of Richard III. Third, More always had an interest in literature and literary style – as his poetry demonstrates – and he enjoyed experimenting with different types and forms of writing, which the study of the classics exposed him to and which the study of rhetoric encouraged. Fourth, and most important, More believed not only that the proper study of the wisdom of the ancients could be shown to be in line with Christian thought, but that such learning stimulated better Christian thinking, posing challenges that resulted in better answers, bringing in new perspectives and demonstrating, if read properly, that a pre-Christian understanding was spread throughout the world, and that the best pagans were ready to convert to Christianity once they were given its message.

PICO AND POEMS

One of More's earliest English works (*c.* 1510) is his translation of the life of Giovanni Pico della Mirandola (1463–1494), written by his nephew, Gianfrancesco, in 1504.[7] Pico is best known to contemporary readers through his *Oration on the Dignity of Man*, often read as one of the central works of humanist thinking that challenged theocentric assumptions that God was at the centre of everything.[8] For More, Pico's life tells a different story, that of a modern saint who lived a life of devotion and died a good death. More translates Gianfrancesco's admission that Pico may not always have seemed like an ideal Christian:

> But in the inward effects of the mind he cleaved to god with very fervent love and devotion. Some time that marvellous alacrity languished and almost fell: and eft again with great strength rose up in to god. In the love of whom he so fervently burned that on a time as he walked with John Francis his nephew in an orchard at Ferrara in the talking of the love of christ he broke out into these words, nephew said he this will I show thee I warn thee keep it secret: the substance that I have left after certain books of mine finished I intend to give out to poor folk and fencing myself with the crucifix, bare foot walking about the world in every town and castle I purpose to preach of christ. Afterward I understand by the especial commandment of god he changed that purpose and appointed to profess himself in the order of friars preachers.[9]

More anticipates probable objections to his work as a translator (as he does when he translates Lucian) and answers them in advance. Pico does not always appear to adhere directly to the faith, but his biographer knows the true state of his mind, making this a hagiography, with Pico as a Christian humanist saint, an

example for others to emulate. Pico acts through proper devotion to God, doing nothing for a worldly audience, which is why he asks his nephew to keep secret his plans to devote his books to the poor. Pico's early death clearly prevented him from carrying out his plan to travel the globe barefoot, preaching as a mendicant friar. For More, Pico resembles an Italian saint like St Francis of Assisi (*c.* 1181–1226), the founder of the order of friars that Pico

Cristofano dell'Altissimo, *Pico della Mirandola*, *c.* 1552–68, oil on canvas.

joins, who was a rich, worldly man who gave everything away to serve the poor. Pico, in More's translation, has become the inspirational Christian humanist, rather than just a humanist. His learning has led to revelation, an understanding that possessions and knowledge can never be enough, and that his duty is to serve God.

Equally, however, there is a critique of Pico, who also emerges as a timorous and withdrawn figure, wary of telling the world what he knows to be true, a pointed contrast to More himself perhaps. Pico has kept his Christian humanist learning hidden and not provided useful service of the state. Only later, through the active intervention of those like More eager to declare the truth, can his real value emerge. Pico is simultaneously an admirable and limited figure, and the traditions he inaugurated and inspired need to be more openly declared and developed by others more committed to public service.

Before the burden of office restricted his time, More was an enthusiastic author of poems in English and Latin. In an early work, *Progymnasmata*, More and the grammarian William Lily (1468?–1522/3) follow Greek precedents and produce a series of rival epigrams in Latin translated from the Greek on a range of subjects, an exercise designed to demonstrate linguistic proficiency. More and Lily are invariably very close in their attempts and the volume is chiefly valuable in demonstrating the significance of the epigram as a poetic form for More. The demands of balancing wit and moral instruction can be shown through More's epigram 'On Self-Indulgence and Lust':

> Si quis ad infernos properet descendere manes,
> Huc iter accelerant, balnea, uina, Venus.
>
> [If anyone is in haste to join the shades of the dead
> below, then baths and wine and the pleasures of love
> shorten the journey thither.][10]

The ironic praise of pleasure in a familiar Latin mode dovetails neatly with More's praise of Lucian in the letter to Thomas Ruthall, as, perhaps, does the rather crueller verse 'On a Man Both Lame and Stupid':

> Clauda tibi mens est, ut pes: natura notasque
> Exterior certas interioris habet.
>
> [Your mind is as lame as your leg, and your external
> condition Gives sure signs of your inner state.][11]

The exercise does not necessarily reflect More's beliefs, although it does serve as a reminder of how robust and cruel sixteenth-century humour could often be.

Between 1500 and 1520 More wrote a large number of Latin epigrams, heavily influenced by the Roman poet Martial (38/41–102/4) and the Italian epigrammist Gian Francesco Poggio Bracciolini (1380–1459), as well as Lucian (who did not write epigrams but whose view of human fallibility had a profound impact on More's early writing). Martial was known for his technical brilliance as well as his ability to shock his readers with striking and startling juxtapositions and frank sexual poems. More's volume, which was often published with Erasmus's epigrams and *Utopia*, is rarely as sexualized as Martial's (although there is one epigram on cunnilingus).[12] Some of the epigrams would not look out of place in Martial's extensive collection, such as 'On an Astrologer Whose Wife Was Lewd':

> Quid inter alta stulte quaeris sydera
> In humo manentis coniugis mores tuae?
> Quid alta spectas? infra id est cui tu times.
> Dum iam tu, agat quid illa, quaeris in polo,
> Haec quae libebat, interim egit in solo.

> [Foolish fellow, why do you search the stars for the character of your wife? Your wife is on the ground. Why do you peer on high? What you are fearful about is down here. While you are asking the heavens what she is doing, she meanwhile managed to do what she liked upon the ground.][13]

Others are witty meditations on fate, especially the inevitability of death, as represented by 'On Fuscus, the Drinker':

> Potando medicus perituros dixit ocellos
> Fusco, qui cum se consuluisset ait:
> Perdere dulcuis est potando, quam ut mea seruem
> Erodenda pigris lumina uermiculis.

> [His physician told Fuscus that drinking would destroy his eyes. When Fuscus had considered the matter, he said, 'I would rather destroy my eyes by drinking than preserve them to be gnawed out by crawling worms.'][14]

The poem most obviously serves as a memento mori, but then we are forced to ask, does this make Fuscus a fool, or a relatively wise man, one who understands the vanities of the world and the transience of life? But, then again, most people would be better off with their eyes than without them, so probably Fuscus is a silly dipsomaniac who cannot look after himself. Or perhaps the poem is not really trying to indicate a moral but is merely a witticism.

Other poems are far more serious, reflections on the subjects that More thought about most often. More was especially interested in tyranny: what made a ruler into a tyrant; how could the signs of creeping tyranny be recognized; and how should subjects behave when confronted with tyranny?[15] Whether the people could ever depose a tyrant was perhaps the most pressing question in the sixteenth century, one that More had to confront after he decided to serve at the court of Henry VIII, a decision which would eventually cost him his life. More's major reflections on tyranny are contained in his life of Richard III (analysed below), but the subject also concerns him in the Latin epigrams, notably in a poem that might be read alongside the epigram on the drunk man about to lose his sight. In 'Death Unassisted Kills Tyrants', one of the longer poems in the volume, More reflects on the suffering experienced by those living under tyranny rather than the tyrant himself:

> You who have been cruelly persecuted at the hands of unjust men, no matter who you are, take hope. Let kindly hope alleviate your sufferings. A turn of fortune will improve your state – like the sun shining through scattered clouds – or the defender of liberty. Death, touched by pity, will put forth her hand, while the tyrant rages, and rescue you. Death will snatch him away too (the more to please you) and will lay him right before your feet. He who was so carried away by his great wealth and his empty pride, he who once upon a time amid his thronging courtiers was so bold, O he will not be fierce, will not cast down from his high place, abandoned, helpless, penniless. What gift has life ever given you to compare with this gift? The tables are turned: the man once so fearsome deserves only a laugh.[16]

Again, the poem is a memento mori, a reminder that all things will pass as nothing can last forever apart from God. The tyrant lives as though he will never die and never have to answer for his crimes, but he has not considered that his flesh is mortal. The drunk man, Fuscus, does not value his eyes because he is so inebriated that he cannot think about his state; here, the unnamed tyrant seems unable to imagine that his terrible reign will come to an end because he thinks that he is immortal. However, it is this false confidence that makes him ridiculous and secures his reputation as a fool rather than as a wise and just ruler. Everyone is relieved when he dies, remembering him with laughter when the fear he inspires has gone. The poem is also simultaneously a reminder of the Sermon on the Mount, that the meek shall inherit the earth (Matthew 5:5), not the mighty, and that the good Christian must place trust not in the world but in the power of God.

Elsewhere there are poems on familiar subjects, some laughing at human deformity, a few that sneer at ugliness, and a number that are casually misogynistic (as well as some that are openly racist), in line with short tales in jest books, a genre that More knew well and tried out, and with which he was associated in popular memory. 'On a Man Who Has a Shrewish Wife at Home' is one of the milder and wittier examples:

> Vxor amice tibi est semper mala: quam male tractas,
> Fit peior, sed fit pessima quando bene.
> Sed bona si moriatur erit, melior tamen id si
> Te faciat uiuo, ast optima si propere.
>
> [My friend, your wife is always bad. When you treat her badly, she gets worse, but when you treat her well, she becomes worst of all. But if she dies, she will be a good wife; better if she dies while you are alive; and best of all if she dies soon.][17]

The poem, nasty as it is, reflects on fortune and chance because, of course, the speaker and reader understand things may not turn out so fortunately for the friend and he may well die before his wife. Putting one's trust in life on earth to work out well is always a perilous enterprise fraught with danger.

The Latin poems also demonstrate that More was extremely interested in popular English culture. Some are translations of English songs, notably the love song simply titled 'Carmen Versum E Cantione Anglica' ('A Poem Translated from an English Song'):

> O Cor triste malis misere immersumque profundis
> Rumpere: sit poenae terminus iste tuae.
> Sanguinolenta tuae dominae tua uulnera pande,
> Illa brui est, quae nos diuidet una duos.
> Quam miser ergo diu sic heu lachrymabo, querarque:
> Mors ades, et tantis horrida solue malis.

> [Break, sad heart, pitiably engulfed in deepest woe. Let this be the end of your punishment. Show your mistress your bloody wounds. It is she only who will presently part us two. Alas, how long shall I in my misery thus weep and complain? Come, dreadful death, and release me from such monstrous woes.][18]

The poem certainly seems of a different order to the more obviously Latin epigrams in the collection, and is derived from a lost English song.[19] A moral could be drawn from this poem with some effort – that fate is fickle? – but most likely this was a poem that appealed to More and which he wanted to translate.

EPIGRAMS

More's epigrams show that he was engaged with English culture as well as Latin and could move easily between the two when it suited him or when necessity dictated (as is also demonstrated in his polemical religious works). Only about 1,500 lines of More's English verse survive, published posthumously in the volume of

English Works (1557). More had been a precocious youth and wrote a number of 'pageant verses' (probably in the early 1490s), poems that were placed underneath 'goodly hanging[s] of fine painted cloth' in his parents' house.[20] These short, pithy verses look forward to the Latin epigrams of the young adult More in both style and substance. A case in point is 'Childhood', presumably displayed below a now-lost image of a child:

> I am called Childhood, in play is all my mind,
> To cast a quoit, a cokstele, [a stick thrown at a cockerel]
> and a ball.
> A top can I set, and drive it in his kind.
> But would to god these hateful books all,
> Were in a fire brent to powder small.
> Than might I lead my life always in play:
> Which life god send me to mine ending day.[21]

Assuming the verse to be authentic, it demonstrates an unusual wisdom and a talent for irony in a youth, as well as an ability to absorb the prevailing representations of life and death. More was clearly a bookish young man and already understood the value of reading, so the desire to spend a whole lifetime in play was one that he had already left behind, assuming he ever indulged in childish play. Yet again there is the realization of the inevitability of death and the need to prepare for it striking suddenly, here demonstrated through the speaker's desire to live with endless play, as if this was the way to live a good life.

It is important to acknowledge, however, that More valued humour and play and did not think that living a good life in preparation for death meant being constantly solemn. Pleasure and humour had their place – as his regard for Lucian demonstrates – especially on festive occasions, which were important events in the lives of everyone in the sixteenth century.[22] More enjoyed the popular culture of jest books enough to write a tale of his own, 'A Merry Jest How a Sergeant Would Learn to Be a Friar', perhaps written for the feast of the Serjeants at Law, 13 November 1503, when his father was elected a serjeant.[23] This light-hearted poem is mainly written in the rhyming dimeters and robust style popularized by the chief poet at Henry VIII's court, John Skelton (*c.* 1460–1529), More demonstrating his understanding of vernacular culture.

The poem opens with a series of examples of people of one mode of life imagining that they can switch to another, aligning the work with the popular genre of 'estates satire' most famously deployed by Geoffrey Chaucer in *The Canterbury Tales*:

When an hatter
Will go smatter,
In philosophy,
Or a pedlar,
Wax a medlar,
In theology,
All that ensue,
Such crafts new,
They drive so far a cast,
That evermore,
They do therefore,
Beshrew themself at last.[24]

Much of the poem's brief narrative works as a shaggy dog story, listing the wealth and pursuits of the rich merchant whom the serjeant is sent to arrest, followed by the serjeant's laborious pursuit of his elusive prey, further suggesting that the poem was intended for oral delivery at an event. The serjeant eventually disguises himself as a friar and gains entrance to the house, but when he tries to arrest the merchant a fight ensues, recounted in lines that resemble Skelton's more demotic poems, such as 'The Tunning of Elynour Rummynge', published in 1521. Skelton describes his unsavoury subject:

> Her loathly leer
> Is nothing clear,
> But ugly of cheer,
> Droopy and drowsy,
> Scurvy and lowsy;
> Her face all bowsy,

John Skelton, woodcut from *Agaynste a comely coystrowne* (c. 1527).

Comely crinkled,
Wonderously wrinkled,
Like a roast pig's ear,
Bristled with hair.[25]

More describes the ungainly fight in equally comic language:

They fell down both at last,
Then on the ground,
Together round,
With many sad stroke,
They roll and rumble,
They tourney & tumble,
Like pigs in a poke.
So long about,
They heave and shove,
Together that at the last,
The maid the wife,
To break the strife,
Hyed them upward fast.[26]

The woman breaking up the fight emphasizes the ineptitude of the combatants, and marks this passage out as the familiar literary motif of the absurd fight, a parody of chivalric battle. The point is continued when she further batters the hapless friar, having pulled down his hood:

While he was blind,
The wench behind,
Lent him on the floor,
Many a iolle [blow]
About the nolle [head],
With a great batylldore [a wooden bat used in washing].[27]

The jest concludes with a moral that 'every man,/ His own craft use',[28] which is surely not to be taken as a fitting conclusion, the energy and enjoyment of the piece lying in its parodic energy and literary imitations.

More appears to have returned to English poetry at the end of his life, an indication of its value for him, which perhaps suggests that he may have written more than is known. According to his biographer William Rastell, he composed two one-stanza poems while in the Tower, verses that are obvious allegories of fate. 'Davy the Dicer' is an imagined monologue of a gambler reflecting on the vicissitudes of fortune:

Long was I lady luck your serving man,
And now have I lost again all that I gate,
Wherefore when I think on you now and then,
And in my mind remember this and that,
You may not blame me though I beshrew your cat,
But in Faith I bless you again a thousand times,
For lending me now some leisure to make rhymes.[29]

It is probably More's best poem and demonstrates what he might have produced had he chosen to write more English verse. The stanza bears at least a passing resemblance to the poems on fortune by Thomas Wyatt (1503–1542), perhaps the well-known sonnet 'Whoso list to hunt' or, more obviously still, 'They flee from me that sometimes did me seek', with its haunting lines and the poignant recollection that Fortune should never be trusted, especially at the court of a tyrant:

They flee from me that sometime did me seek
With naked foot, stalking in my chamber.
I have seen them gentle, tame, and meek,
That now are wild and do not remember

That sometime they put themself in danger
To take bread at my hand; and now they range,
Busily seeking with a continual change.

Thanked be fortune it hath been otherwise
Twenty times better; but once in special,
In thin array after a pleasant guise,
When her loose gown from her shoulders did fall,
And she me caught in her arms long and small;
Therewithall sweetly did me kiss
And softly said, 'Dear heart, how like you this?'[30]

Wyatt, like More, was imprisoned by the paranoid Henry VIII, although he escaped the executioner's axe.

Wyatt's portrayal of fickle women perhaps refers to real relationships, in which case their leaving him was probably the result of political machinations given the importance of marriage as a means of advancement and allegiance.[31] Equally, the familiar image of Fortune is presented, invariably represented as an attractive woman, either blindfolded or simply indifferent, spinning her wheel at random so that some receive great riches and gifts, while others are punished for no apparent reason. Wyatt thanks Fortune that 'it hath been otherwise,' which alerts readers to his current miserable state, the memory of past joys making the present even less bearable. Things may improve, but who can possibly know?

More's image of the dicer desperately changing his plans as Fortune turns against him (beshrewing the cat means cursing his current situation and changing it immediately) is similar to Wyatt's. It is surely redolent of More's incarceration and impending execution after his worldly success, and, given More's often expressed contempt for gambling as a worthless and often dangerous pastime, connotes sadness as powerfully as Wyatt's sexualized image of the beautiful lover who suddenly disappears. Perhaps, More

is suggesting, he should have gambled more; perhaps it would have made no difference to his eventual fate anyway. The wistful concluding line may be a genuine lament for a lack of time to write poetry, as well as providing a sense that the doomed man must do something worthwhile in his last days. It can also be read in

Hans Holbein the Younger, *Thomas Wyatt*, *c.* 1535–7, black and coloured chalks, pen and ink on paper.

terms of More's first extant poem, a reminder that there comes a time when play has to end.

TYRANNY AND HISTORY

Play ends with death, and so does the 'stage-play' of life, a motif to which More returns frequently through his oeuvre (and a favourite with many humanists), from his earliest translations of Lucian to his final ruminations in the Tower. Men and women are costumed by Fortune, given roles that they must play through life, but 'when the time for the pageant was past each one returned his trappings, and leaving aside both his clothes and his body, became what he was before, no different from his neighbor.'[32] For More, the prudent and educated man performs his role in the stage-play, avoiding disrupting it by pointing out its absurdity. To do so would be to his own mortal peril.

This lesson is brought out clearly in perhaps the most famous passage of More's *History of King Richard III*:

> in a stage play all the people know right well, that he that playeth the Soudan [Sultan] is percase a souter [shoemaker]. Yet if one should can so little good, to show out of season what acquaintance he hath with him, and call him by his own name while he standeth in his majesty, one of his tormentors might hap break his head, and worthy for marring of the play. And so they said that these matters be Kings' games, as it were stage plays, and for the more part played upon scaffolds. In which poor men be but the lookers on. And they that wise be, will meddle no farther. For they that sometime step up and play with them, when they cannot play their parts, they disorder the play and do themself no good.[33]

More's hero of the piece, his former master, John Morton (at the time Bishop of Ely), plays his part to perfection, deftly avoiding death at the hands of Richard III in order to use his rhetorical prowess to convince the tyrant's erstwhile ally, the Duke of Buckingham, to rebellion. As More and his readers well knew, this rebellion was a failure, but Morton would go on to help smooth the path for the invasion of the man who would become Henry VII, becoming his Lord Chancellor and Archbishop of Canterbury. This deviousness is not just allowable but encouraged; More sees it as the only way to navigate the political tides of statesmanship while retaining a sense of integrity.

The History of King Richard III covers the tumultuous months of 1483, a year of three kings, including the death of Edward IV, the brief reign of his young son Edward V and the accession of the former Lord Protector, Richard, Duke of Gloucester, who becomes Richard III. These and the other figures in More's *History* are presented as stock characters – Edward IV is a fine but decadent king, who lets his court go to rot in his final years. Edward V is an innocent victim. And Richard is a scheming, ambitious tyrant, unnatural in his form and methods.

More composed the *History* at the height of his engagement with humanist scholarship; participating in the *ars historica* might have been considered an essential part of More's humanist training (alongside translation), and he wrote the book simultaneously in Latin and English.[34] From internal evidence, it is clear that More began writing his *History* around 1513 and had put down his pen on the project by 1518. Those were transformative years for More, who in that time went from undersheriff of London to a king's councillor, as well as from a lesser-known young English humanist to a scholar of pan-European standing, thanks to *Utopia*. Shortly thereafter, Henry VIII would begin writing his response to Luther, undoubtedly with More's assistance. There was little time, then, to dedicate to finishing his history of the short reign of Richard III.

More was interested in the project of writing history. In the same year that he began writing *Richard III*, he read an epic poem by the French humanist Germain de Brie, recounting the events of the 1512 naval battle that had seen the destruction of the French *Cordelière* and English *Regent*. More lambasted de Brie for falsifying his narrative to glorify both France and warfare, arguing that 'it is not true, it is not a history,' and asking rhetorically, 'Let historians begin to show either prejudice or favouritism, and who will there be to lend any credence at all to histories?'[35]

In his own *History*, More is keen to demonstrate that, unlike de Brie, he had spoken to witnesses of the events described, and he hedged his bets by explicitly reporting public opinion, rather than claiming it for fact. For instance, More prefaces the controversial passage detailing the murder of Edward V and his brother in the Tower of London by declaring that 'I shall rehearse you the dolorous end of those babes, not after every way that I have heard, but after that way that I have so heard by such men and by such means as methinketh it were hard but it should be true.' He repeats that this 'I have learned of them that much knew and little cause had to lie.'[36] That being said, in adherence with the practice of the humanist *ars historica*, More's dedication to truth was no barrier to invention. Quite the contrary: like his classical predecessors and humanist contemporaries, More invents long speeches for the characters in his history that he could never have heard or seen recorded. The truth he seeks to serve in his *History* is a higher moral truth rather than the bare facts of the past.

In the opening pages of the *History*, Edward IV gives a lengthy deathbed speech, warning his nobles against falling into 'great variance' in the reign of his young son, and reminding them of the affinity between them, which ought to keep them in concord. 'Such a pestilent serpent is ambition and desire of vainglory and sovereignty,' the dying king warns prophetically, 'which among states where he once entereth creepeth forth so far till with

Anonymous, *Richard III*, late 16th century, oil on panel.

division and variance he turneth all to mischief – first longing to be next the best, afterward equal with the best, and at last chief and above the best.'[37] Though Richard usurps the throne, Edward's speech – which More could not have recorded from memory or report – suggests that it is conflict between the king's councillors which allows for his rise.

Richard is cast unambiguously as the villain, an ambitious, paranoid tyrant who does not hesitate to murder his own young

The burning of the *Cordelière* and the *Regent* at the Battle of Saint-Mathieu, 1512, from a French manuscript version by Pierre Choque of Germain de Brie, *Chordigerae navis conflagration* (1514–15).

nephews in pursuit of power. This allows More to further ruminate on the nature of tyranny, as well as what one ought to do in response to it, which he channels largely through his hero, Morton. Tyranny, fuelled by self-interest, serves to break apart the commonwealth; 'all the bands broken that binden man and man together, without any respect of God or the world', demonstrated by the murders of the 'princes'.[38] Working against tyranny, then, is essential public service, even when it means fostering rebellion or inviting invasion. Both Richard and Morton play parts, one to the downfall of the commonwealth, one to its benefit.

Does this mean More thinks it is justifiable to overthrow a king when he is a tyrant and usurper, as Richard is presented? The evidence of his early works would suggest that he does. Though he does not get past 1483 in either version of the *History*, there is no question that he was intending to welcome the accession of Henry VII, even if just as a precursor to the reign of his son, Henry VIII. Henry Tudor exiled in France, raised troops against Richard III and defeated him in battle, where Richard was killed. Though much propagandistic work was prepared to justify this as right and just, it is difficult to ignore the fact that it was an invasion and a usurpation with even less legitimacy than Richard's.

More had addressed the question, at least somewhat, in his translations of Lucian, which had included an original essay on tyrannicide. Using a classical case, in which a man had claimed the reward for killing a tyrant – as his murder of the king's son had led to the tyrant's suicide – More argued that the man was not deserving of the reward (as he had not killed the tyrant directly), but he did not make the argument that tyrannicide was wrong. He describes the successful killer of a tyrant in positive terms as a 'resourceful man, one not only strong-handed but (muchmore) strong-hearted; able in stratagem rather than force; one who knows how to lay plots, hide his traps, make the most of opportunities'. More's speech admits that, if the man had killed the tyrant directly, 'I would not complain; on the contrary I would praise and admire you.'[39]

As More makes clear in *Richard III*, Richard is not properly king. English kingship, More is at pains to outline, requires the consensus and consent of the people, which Richard fabricates in his *History* but does not actually hold. As More writes in his Latin poems, 'the consent of the people both bestows and withdraws sovereignty,' for 'he ought to have command not one instant longer than his subjects wish,' a sentiment repeated in the *History*.[40] Lacking, then, the consent of the people, Richard III is not actually king; nor is any monarch who had once ruled by consensus of the people, but who descends into tyranny.

DEATH AND JUDGEMENT

The Last Things, written circa 1522, has often been seen to mark a transition in More's writing, as he turned from 'the humanistic interests of the early years (1500–1520) to the polemical and theological concerns of his later life (1520–1535)'.[41] In this meditative English work, More explores the four things connected with the end of life and the start of the afterlife: death, judgement, hell and heaven. In concentrating again on the *ars moriendi*, the work continues his earlier concerns with how to live a good life and to prepare for a good death, as well as looking forward to his concentration on theology and ecclesiology as he sought to explain and defend the role of the Church as it came under siege.

The treatise, unfinished as it was, was published in 1522, just as More stepped up his duties as the king's councillor. It consists of two parts, which eloquently make a series of points familiar in medieval eschatological traditions, thinking about death and judgement. The first part provides an overview of life and death, arguing that pursuing virtue makes people happiest and provides true pleasure; that the pleasures of the world and the flesh are eventually painful, and that spiritual pleasure is lasting; that all philosophy should concentrate on death, as life itself is a long disease; and that the Devil tempts the dying most effectively. The second part, which is more vivid and memorable, outlines the seven deadly sins, one of the central features of the medieval art of death, starting with pride, the worst of the sins and the one that caused Lucifer's fall from heaven, and concluding with gluttony, before the treatise abruptly stops.

Throughout More writes with the vigour of a powerful sermon, a genre to which his work is heavily indebted.[42] In the first section he constantly reminds readers that life is always a form of death, and that we are surrounded by signs that we should think about the afterlife, not the earthly one:

Michael Volgemut, 'The Dance of Death', woodcut from Hartmann Schedel's *Nuremberg Chronicle* (1493).

> Consider also that all our swaddling and tending with warm clothes, and daily medicines, yet can our bodies not bear themself, but that almost half our time ever in 24 hours, we be fain to fall in a swoon which we call sleep, and there lie like dead stocks by a long space ere we come to our self again: in so much that among all wise men of old, it is agreed that sleep is the very image of death.[43]

From the cradle to the grave we are dying, and whatever we do we cannot escape the inevitability of our demise (in pointed contrast to the inviolability of our souls). Sleep, another inevitability in life, serves as a further reminder of death, as the sleeping look like the dead and the unconsciousness of sleep may be the closest experience we can have to the reality of death.

The second part is often more striking still, especially when More inserts anecdotes. In his discussion of covetousness he includes a story of a desperate prisoner in Newgate awaiting execution, probably based on his experience as a lawyer:

> I remember me of a thief once cast at Newgate, that cut a purse at the bar when he should be hanged on the morrow. And when he was asked why he did so, knowing that he should die so shortly, the desperate wretch said, that it did his heart good, to be lord of that purse, one night yet. And in good faith me-thinketh as much as we wonder at him, yet see we many that do much like, of whom we nothing wonder at all. I let pass old priests that sew for vowsons of younger priests' benefices. I let passe old men that houe [stare] and gape to be executors to some that be younger than themselves: whose goods, if they would fall, they reckon would do them good to have in their keeping yet one year ere they die.[44]

It is a powerful and affective moment in the narrative. The thief would rather be mighty for a day and lose his life than do the right thing. On a basic level the thief demonstrates the nature of contemporary life in London. People are immoral and have no regard for their fellow citizens, as they have become greedy and selfish. This problem is surely a result of human sin, but it may also be facilitated by envy, the gap between the haves and the have-nots, as the city expands and grows ever more wealthy. Whatever the cause, people's souls are placed in danger as a result. More is careful to widen the significance of the incident so that it cannot inspire complacency in the law-abiding reader. Using the familiar rhetorical trope of *occupatio* (emphasizing something by pretending that it is not important), More reminds the reader that it is not just the criminal who is guilty of covetousness: priests are also afflicted by this sin, as are those who seek to gain control of or inherit money and goods from another's estate. Just as the doomed criminal refuses to repent because he simply wanted to be wealthy for a day, so the old men, whose time on earth is fast approaching its end, risk losing their afterlife in heaven because they would rather be rich for a short time than forgo riches. More reminds us that it is not just the unfortunate and those at the bottom of the social scale who exhibit envy and greed, but many who refuse to imagine that they are committing deadly sins that God will inevitably punish.

TWO

More and Erasmus

More's visits to Europe and, more importantly, his correspondence, made him part of a group of intellectuals, statesmen, writers, publishers and theologians, all influenced by humanism and determined – with one temporary exception – to defend the Church against Lutheran attacks. The most important members of this Republic of Letters, all of whom appear in More's writings, were Pieter Gillis, an intellectual printer, lawyer and civil servant based in Antwerp; Maarten van Dorp, a theologian who taught at the University of Leuven and who was briefly attracted to the writings of the reformers before his friends persuaded him to reaffirm his commitment to the Church; Thomas Lupset, an English churchman and scholar; Cuthbert Tunstall, Bishop of Durham and another leading Catholic reformer; and, undoubtedly his closest friend and intellectual companion, Desiderius Erasmus, the pivotal figure in the group and, in effect, its leader.

Erasmus, a humanist scholar, priest, Bible translator, satirist and philosopher, was a byword in his lifetime for the intellectual possibilities open to men of letters after the advent of the Renaissance and the rediscovery of classical writings. He was the oldest of this particular group and the figure who connected everyone through his often exhausting travels around Europe, as well as shared publication projects, debates and extensive correspondence. Numerous letters between More and Erasmus survive, but these are only a fraction of those that they are known to have sent to each other.

REPUBLIC OF LETTERS

More and Erasmus first met in 1499 and continued their active friendship until More's death 36 years later. They shared similar intellectual and spiritual concerns, finding classical learning an inspiration as they thought it was in line with the teachings of the Church, and they were both eager to rethink Christianity in line with the new developments of humanism. Both thought that retranslating the Bible and the writings of the Church Fathers in line with new philological developments was essential if God's message was not to be obscured and distorted, and they had little time for those who thought that the best way to stave off the Reformation was to retreat into the ancient practices of the Church and not admit that change might be required to revivify the Christian message. Both were keen adherents of the study and practice of rhetoric, and they thought that the dominance of dialectical logic in the study of the scriptures in the medieval university had led to arcane and pointless speculation rather than useful practical instruction in the possible ways of devotion. They disagreed when More felt it his duty to serve Henry VIII, Erasmus clearly indicating in their correspondence that he would have preferred More to continue his writing and thinking and to live a peripatetic scholarly life, as Erasmus did. They disagreed about Martin Luther: for More, as his polemical works demonstrate, Luther was the agent of the Devil seeking to destroy God's Church; for Erasmus, Luther was an important figure with innovative ideas who took them rather too far, as their debate over the freedom of the will demonstrates.[1]

Erasmus was initially embarrassed by his early encounter with the much younger More, as More had been briefed to prepare

Hans Holbein the Younger, *Desiderius Erasmus*, 1523, oil and tempera on panel.

some writing for Prince Henry and he had not. However, he soon got over his discomfort and by the autumn of that year they had begun a correspondence that was to last until More's death. In a much later letter (23 July 1519) written to Ulrich von Hutten (1488–1523), a poet and satirist who had sympathies for Luther, Erasmus provides his friend with a long description of More:

> in shape and stature More is not a tall man, but not remarkably short, all his limbs being so symmetrical that no deficiency is observed in this respect . . . His countenance answers to his character, having an expression of kind and friendly cheerfulness with a little air of raillery. To speak candidly, it is a face more expressive of pleasantry than of gravity or dignity . . . I have never seen any person less fastidious in his choice of food. As a young man, he was by preference a water-drinker, a practice he derived from his father. But, not to give annoyance to others, he used at table to conceal this habit from his guests by drinking, out of a pewter vessel, either small beer almost as weak as water, or plain water . . . His voice is neither loud nor excessively low, but of a penetrating tone. It has nothing in it melodious or soft, but is simply suitable for speech, as he does not seem to have any natural talent for singing, though he takes pleasure in music of every kind. His articulation is wonderfully distinct, being equally free from hurry and from hesitation.
>
> He likes to be dressed simply, and does not wear silk, or purple, or gold chains, except when it is not allowable to dispense with them. He cares marvellously little for those formalities, which with ordinary people are the test of politeness; and as he does not exact these ceremonies from others, so he is not scrupulous in observing them himself, either on occasions of meeting or at

entertainments, though he understands how to use them, if he thinks proper to do so; but he holds it to be effeminate and unworthy of a man to waste much of his time on such trifles.

He was formerly rather disinclined to Court life and to any intimacy with princes, having always special hatred of tyranny and a great fancy for equality; whereas you will scarcely find any Court so well-ordered, as not to have much bustle and ambition and pretence and luxury, or to be free from tyranny in some form or other. He could not even be tempted to Henry the Eighth's Court without great trouble, although nothing could be desired more courteous or less exacting than this Prince. He is naturally fond of liberty and leisure; but as he enjoys a holiday when he has it, so whenever business requires it, no one is more vigilant or more patient.

He seems to be born and made for friendship, of which he is the sincerest and most persistent devotee. Neither is he afraid of that multiplicity of friends . . . he has found many sincere friends, whose characters are suited to his own, he is so delighted with their society and conversation, that he seems to find in these the chief pleasure of life, having an absolute distaste for tennis and dice and cards, and the other games with which the mass of gentlemen beguile the tediousness of Time. It should be added that, while he is somewhat neglectful of his own interest, no one takes more pains in attending to the concerns of his friends. What more need I say? If anyone requires a perfect example of true friendship, it is in More that he will best find it.

In company his extraordinary kindness and sweetness of temper are such as to cheer the dullest spirit, and alleviate the annoyance of the most trying circumstances.

> From boyhood he was always so pleased with a joke, that it might seem that jesting was the main object of his life; but with all that, he did not go so far as buffoonery, nor had ever any inclination to bitterness.[2]

Erasmus's testimony is noteworthy for many reasons, not only as it helps explain why and how he valued More's character and why he set such store on their friendship, but because it tells us a great deal about early modern friendship, the ways in which both Erasmus and More conducted their affairs and, equally importantly, how they liked to be seen to be acting.[3] More was an attractive figure for Erasmus, the description here perhaps tinged with homoeroticism, but what is really important is how easy and relaxed Erasmus suggests More feels in the company of others, a sign of true friendship. As an ancient ideal, one that acquired great significance in Renaissance Europe, friendship stood out as a relationship between equals, a horizontal bond between disinterested people (usually men) who could interact as equals, in a society constructed around vertical, hierarchical relationships (rank, status, marriage, servitude and so on).[4] Erasmus signals that More is especially good at friendship, and that he cares very little for ceremony and tradition, placing emphasis instead on the substance of thoughts and actions rather than the appearance of them. Given Erasmus's desire to represent himself in his letters, and his use of letters to represent his nature, there is an obviously self-interested motive at work here, as Erasmus demonstrates that his circle do not care for the stuffy and pointless formality that passes for sophistication in Europe, but are interested solely in discussing serious ideas with serious like-minded people – that is, their friends. While others waste time on trifles, More and Erasmus exchange serious ideas and think matters through.

Erasmus further confirms that More is light-hearted and understands the serious nature of comedy or play, a feature of his character and reputation that survived long after his death. More is never trivial – and, by implication, neither is Erasmus – and he eschews gambling and foolish pastimes (an important issue in *Utopia*). He is prepared to join in to put others at their ease – and so enable them to join in the conversation to better effect – but he never indulges in excessive pleasure because it does not interest him and detracts from the true pleasure of life, intellectual conversation. The description of More's voice as being clear and not too loud is yet more testimony of how he behaves and how he has shaped his natural qualities to the best effect.

It is also worth noting that Erasmus describes More as someone who does not put their own interests first, but does what suits the group (of friends) best. In obvious ways this is a virtue, although there is surely also more than a hint of criticism, as he perhaps allows the needs and desires of others to obscure his own. Erasmus surely has in mind the decision More made, recounted in the previous paragraph, to serve Henry VIII and put his writing to one side. In 1519 Henry had not yet emerged as the tyrannical figure he became after the annulment of his marriage to Catherine of Aragon, so Erasmus's comment that More had a 'special hatred of tyranny' does not have the force it would have done had he made it in the 1530s. The point here is that Erasmus regrets that More has compromised his ideals and put himself in service rather than being free to speak his mind and nurture his ideals.[5] The description also works as a series of reflections on how an individual should balance their own interests, those of others and their duties to the state, the concerns outlined in *Utopia*.

FRIENDSHIP AND LUCIAN

The friendship of More and Erasmus was carefully represented in a number of published works. In 1509, ten years after they first met, Erasmus published his witty exploration of wisdom and foolishness, *The Praise of Folly* (*Stultitiae laus* or *Moriae encomium*), the work that was to cement the public nature of their private friendship. Erasmus's playfully serious text has the female figure of Folly attack and praise minor and major forms of poor behaviour: from the excesses of lovers to abuses of the Church, from the absurdities of pedantic scholars to the misery caused by corrupt officials. Erasmus's dedicatory letter to More explains that, forced to ride back in company after his stay at More's house, he decided to amuse himself thinking of his friendship and the pleasure that More's companionship gives him. As a result he thinks about a subject related to their 'common interests' and he decides to amuse himself with the praise of folly, signalling that both enjoy jokes and word games:

> What sort of a goddess Athene put that notion into your head, you may well ask. In the first place, it was your own family name of More, which is as near to the Greek word for folly, *moria*, as you are far from it in fact, and everyone agrees that you couldn't be farther removed. Then I had an idea that no one would think so well of this *jeu d'esprit* of mine as you, because you always take such delight in jokes of this kind, that is, if I don't flatter myself, jokes which aren't lacking in learning and wit.[6]

The first draft of *Folly* was, in fact, completed at More's house (although it is possible that the text we have has been heavily revised and bears little resemblance to his first efforts), so the letter is a partial fiction, written to highlight the friendship of the two European men of letters.[7] In suggesting that the work is largely a shared enterprise which has developed from their intellectual and personal interests, Erasmus is advertising their conversation, based on wit and insight, as a means of instruction, from which a diligent reader can learn a huge amount. The title can be read as 'Praise of More' as well as folly, casting them both as wise fools speaking truth to power. The work might be described as light and frivolous, but it is apparent to an alert reader that it is nothing of the sort and is a serious exploration of foolishness and vice that seeks to expose the evils of European society, indicating that these can be solved if wise fools like the humanists are employed to tackle them (which further explains why Erasmus was so disappointed by More's decision to serve Henry VIII).

Erasmus anticipates criticism of his book, and acts to deflect it:

> There may well be plenty of critical folk rushing in to slander it, some saying that my bit of nonsense is too frivolous for a theologian and others that it has a sarcastic bite which ill becomes Christian decorum. They will clamour that I'm reviving Old Comedy or Lucian, carping and complaining about everything. Well, those who are offended by frivolity and fun in a thesis may kindly consider that mine is not the first example of this; the same thing has often been done by famous authors in the past.[8]

Erasmus continues to list several serious authors who have had to endure criticism for using humour to correct widespread ills: Homer, Vergil, Ovid and Polycrates among them. In doing so he casts himself and More as the inheritors of classical learning – in particular, satire – using sophisticated literary forms and style to force readers to think more carefully about the many things that they have taken for granted far too easily and which need to be challenged and corrected.

He suggests that ill-educated or philistine readers will dismiss his work as 'Old Comedy', like the plays of Aristophanes and his contemporaries. In doing so they are only showing their ignorance as such plays satirized absurdities and vices and were extremely serious works of literature, notably *The Clouds*, which ridiculed the impractical ideas of philosophers, and *Lysistrata*, a vigorous anti-war farce. Humorous literature, as More and Erasmus are here shown to realize, is often the most serious form of writing.

Erasmus also suggests that he may be criticized for imitating Lucian, the Greek satirist who exposed the follies of his contemporaries, and whose works were the main literary model for *Folly*. Lucian of Samosata wrote a number of satirical dialogues, as well as a novel, *A True Story*, parodying many of the incredible stories in Homer's epic poems. Lucian's satires expose the absurdities of his contemporaries, indicting philosophers alongside ordinary, gullible people who have not the wit or imagination to see through the charlatans who dupe them.

More, along with Erasmus, was a great admirer of Lucian, enjoying his ironic, witty style and clever turns of thought. For More, Lucian was a model to follow, balancing a contempt for the world with a desire to correct human folly, and always expressing a benign faith in human perfectibility.[9] Both More and Erasmus translated a selection of Lucian's satires that were published in 1506, three years before Erasmus published *Folly*.

More prefaces his edition of translations of four of Lucian's satires with a dedicatory letter to Thomas Ruthall, Bishop of Durham and significant crown servant, known to both More and Erasmus as a fine example of someone who could square the often conflicting demands of devotion to Church and king.[10] More defends his subject choice, arguing that St John Chrysostom, one of More's favourite saints, also admired Lucian, who inspired his own work, especially the first one in More's volume, *Cynicus*, a dialogue which demonstrates that the simple life is best, a message in line with a Christian suspicion of worldly wealth and success:

> So much did this dialogue delight him that he introduced a large part of it into a homily he composed on the Gospel of St. John. And not without reason: for what should have pleased that grave and truly Christian man more than this dialogue in which, while the severe life of Cynics, satisfied with little, is defended and the soft, enervating luxury of voluptuaries denounced, by the same token Christian simplicity, temperance and frugality, and finally that straight and narrow path which leads to life eternal, are praised?[11]

More continues, arguing in good Christian humanist fashion, that while many will be sceptical, the works of pagans have much to teach us if we read them correctly in the light of true worship. *Philopseudes*, a dialogue about telling the truth and lying, is a case in point:

> For what difference does it make to me what a pagan thinks about those articles contained in the principal mysteries of the Christian faith? Surely the dialogue will teach us this lesson: that we should put no trust in magic and that we should eschew superstition, which obtrudes everywhere under the guise of religion. It teaches us also that we should live a life less distracted by anxiety; less fearful, that is, of any gloomy and superstitious untruths.[12]

More uses his skill as a rhetorician and lawyer to establish an objection, only to demolish it as he answers the question he poses, making his point more powerfully than if he had simply asserted his case. The dialogues of Lucian are, accordingly, simply one example of useful and instructive writings written by those who lived as good a life as they could, not having the benefits of Christian revelation. Lucian's dialogue concludes that adhering to common sense provides 'a powerful antidote to such poisons in truth [lies] and in sound reason brought to bear everywhere', and that 'as long as we make use of this, none of these empty, foolish lies will disturb our peace.'[13]

Folly is a Lucianic text, the product of Erasmus and More's shared enthusiasm for the Greek satirist, a good literary model for the two humanists to follow in their writing because he balanced a comic acceptance of human foibles with a satiric edge designed to make people look more closely and critically at the limitations of their own behaviour. Erasmus is clear that he has chosen Lucian because his benign style enables him to make his message more accessible and palatable to a wide audience and, therefore, more likely to hit home. Erasmus explains what he is doing in *Folly*, a description of his approach that we have no reason to doubt is to be taken at face value:

> I have not only refrained from naming anyone but have also moderated my style so that the sensible reader will easily understand that my intention was to give pleasure, not pain. Nowhere have I stirred up the hidden cesspool of crime as Juvenal did; the ridiculous rather than the squalid was what I set out to survey. Finally, if anyone is still unappeased by all I have said, he should at least remember that there is merit in being attacked by Folly, for when I made her the narrator I had to maintain her character in appropriate style.[14]

Lucian is preferred to the more acerbic and aggressive Roman satirist Juvenal (*c.* 55–128 CE), whose excoriating poems were hilarious, obsessively focused on vice and pollution, and aimed to demolish his targets. Erasmus's aim is to lure readers in and then have them reflect on what they have read and how it might relate to who they are and what they do.

Furthermore, in adopting a Greek author rather than a Latin one as their inspiration, More and Erasmus were showing that they wished to push humanist study beyond the familiar Latin names then enshrined in the school and university curriculum. Accordingly, Erasmus's *Folly* is claimed as – almost – a jointly authored project, and More's *Utopia* is promoted by Erasmus in its paratexts, the first book perhaps mimicking the Republic of Letters of the European humanists of the More–Erasmus circle, through the representation of the lively debates taking place in Cardinal Morton's household. It is easy to understand why Erasmus might have been so dismayed when More abandoned the Republic of Letters for political service, and the complicated, questioning style of his early humanist work for the combative polemic of his theological treatises.

FOLLY AND FRICTION

More, like Erasmus, saw *Folly* as a major work that demonstrated much of what they were trying to achieve in their writings. A sense of the tricky and unsettling nature of Erasmus's constantly shifting text can be obtained through his discussion of learning and the scholarly professions, which starts by defining folly one way before radically shifting our understanding. After listing the divisions of learning, Folly argues:

> The most highly valued amongst these learned disciplines, however, are those which come closest to common sense, or rather, to folly. Theologians go hungry, scientists are cold-shouldered, astrologers laughed at, and dialecticians ignored; only 'the doctor is man worth many men.'

> And the more ignorant, reckless, and thoughtless a doctor is, the higher his reputation soars even amongst powerful princes . . . Next to doctors the petty lawyers take second place. Maybe they ought to be the first, but the philosophers are all agreed that theirs is a profession for asses and are always laughing at them . . . yet these asses can settle matters large and small if they give the word, and their estates multiply, while the theologian who has combed through his bookcases in order to master the whole of divinity nibbles at a dry bean and carries on a non-stop war with bugs and lice.
>
> Thus the happier branches of knowledge are those which are more nearly related to folly, and by far the happiest men are those who have no traffic at all with any kind of learning and follow Nature for their guide.[15]

The passage starts off as a familiar satire of the pointed contrast between worldly values and learning, as Folly argues that true scholarship is not recognized and leads to a lifetime of poverty, while charlatanism is ludicrously well rewarded. Even at this point, however, there is a possible complication if we remember that More was a lawyer and made his living in the common law courts, which refers us to the title and the opening epistle, equating More and Folly. Is Erasmus laughing at More's profession and, if so, is that because his friend has been over-indulged? Or is this ironic, pointing out More's dedication to serving others and neglect of his own interests, as the letter to von Hutten indicated was central to More's character?

There is surely also a shift towards the end of the paragraph with the description of the theologian trawling through his bookcases to find out obscure pieces of knowledge to help him make his argument. Such endeavour is not being endorsed by Erasmus even as Folly seems adamant that the theologian's work is valuable and neglected. Erasmus's point is undoubtedly that theologians have devalued their labours through arguing over tiny points of little interest or relevance to ordinary Christians, rather than working to elucidate the mysteries of the faith to a wider audience, which is, after all, what they are supposed to be doing. So when in the next paragraph Folly turns to Nature and claims that the happiest branches of knowledge are those which follow Nature, we are not quite sure how to understand this shift. Who, here, are wise and who are foolish? On the one hand, we might condemn the doctors and lawyers who make money and seem to have realized that people are naturally gullible and can be exploited for profit; on the other hand, the theologians are not really serving anyone but themselves and their pursuit of knowledge might seem to be unnatural. Perhaps the point is that all are fools: one group are successful fools, the other, unsuccessful, which suggests that the first are wise fools, the second, just fools.

It is a powerful satire that forces the reader to think about what they know and how life might be organized rather better. The implied answer, naturally, is that people need to value humanism and humanist study, which for Erasmus means learning from the humanists and their writings. For More, who would seem not to have shared his friend's confidence that good scholarship on its own was enough, that might involve seeking out the courts to provide proper counsel to those in positions of power.[16]

Folly, as Erasmus anticipated, had its share of detractors. One was Maarten van Dorp who, inspired by the scepticism of theologians in his home town (Leuven) for the humanist project, as well as Protestant attacks on Church abuses, argued that Erasmus's enthusiasm for classical culture went too far and risked being counterproductive.[17] In an open letter to Dorp written in 1515 that circulated widely in manuscript, More countered

Dorp's criticisms. Opening by professing his friendship and signalling to readers that Dorp was part of Erasmus's circle, More admonished him for being foolhardy in his comments and breaking the bonds of fellowship. More urges reconciliation but is clear that he will not tolerate what he regards as unfair and unfounded criticism of Erasmus. More's approach is in line with the Lucianic style and tone that he and Erasmus adopted at the time, seeking to draw Dorp back into the fold and to correct his errors:

> I am not particularly troubled by the way that you carp at the *Folly*, inveigh at the poets, snarl at all the grammarians, disapprove of his annotations on scripture, or judge that a training in Greek literature is simply irrelevant. In these matters, without offending anyone, everyone has a right to his own point of view. Besides, you have so far presented your case on these topics in such a way that I have no doubt that many arguments occur to everyone while reading your letter which ought to be stated for the opposite viewpoint. In fact, far from considering that you have said too much on any of these topics, on a number I find a good deal left unsaid . . .
>
> On the other hand, it certainly disturbed me a good deal that you seem to handle Erasmus in a way that is worthy of neither of you. You treat him sometimes as if you despise him, sometimes as if you regard him with haughty derision, sometimes as if you are not so much offering advice as chastising him like a stern uncle or humorless censor, and lastly as if you are deliberately twisting the meaning of his words to get all the theologians and even all the universities, as they are called, up in arms against him.[18]

The criticism builds carefully and logically from More's initial assertion that he is not greatly troubled by Dorp's comments and that he wished he had written rather more, so that they could have a proper debate about an important subject, to the second paragraph in which he argues that Dorp is simply insulting Erasmus, demeaning him and not treating him with the respect that he deserves as a friend and established scholar and thinker. More concludes that Dorp is, in fact, guilty of inciting hatred against Erasmus, so that he is treated far worse than an ordinary neglected scholar described in *Folly*; rather, as an enemy of the people. While the first paragraph acknowledges that everyone has the right to a point of view, the second attempts to demonstrate that Dorp has indulged in comment that borders on defamation and libel (as a lawyer, More knew how to deploy legal threats). Not only does Dorp treat Erasmus like an old fool, but he writes as though he were lacking humour, one of the key features of *Folly*, so More is implying that Dorp has read that work very poorly and is indeed one of *Folly*'s legitimate targets. Furthermore, Dorp writes as though Erasmus were a censor, like one of the theologians who sought to prohibit challenging books, whereas Erasmus was eager to learn as much as possible from as many sources as possible to arrive at the truth. Indeed, More is suggesting, Dorp contradicts himself in attacking the range of Erasmus's learning and then treating him as if he were a thinker who sought to censor material with which he disagreed.

The exchange concluded more or less amicably, but it pointed out important disagreements over religion, ones that later divided More and Erasmus. More's letter mounts a robust defence of Erasmian humanism, and the necessity of learning Greek to translate the Bible better than it has been in the past. Erasmus, More argues, is working hard to reform scholarship for the benefit of everyone, and is using the correct scholarly resources that he requires, as Latin texts cannot be relied on any longer. Dorp has become one of the foolish theologians who are offended by *Folly* because they cannot grasp the subtle arguments of this challenging book:

> For one proof that Folly pleases only the learned is simply that only the learned understand her, which indeed was perhaps why those two or three theologians that Folly upset became angry: on the basis of what others told them, they thought she said more than she did, while perhaps if they themselves understood what was actually said they would not feel provoked.[19]

More is admonishing Dorp for his limited understanding and failure to think matters through before he ventures into print, indicating that there is a danger that he will become an opponent of the Erasmian circle rather than a member of it, if he is not careful. More points out that Dorp has not objected to the satires of Gerard Geldenhouwer of Nijmegen (1482–1542), another member of their circle who eventually converted to Protestantism. Geldenhouwer, according to More, is just as critical of monks and friars as Erasmus, as he points out their 'pride, luxury, ignorance, drinking bouts, gluttony, lust, and hypocrisy' in exactly the same way as Erasmus does.[20] Accordingly, Dorp is hoist by his own petard and guilty of double standards based on his religious affiliation, exactly the sort of double-thinking that Erasmus is seeking to counter.

More concludes by demonstrating that to his mind Dorp has failed to understand *Folly* and that his purported advice is simply pointless. More tries to make Dorp look as ridiculous as the targets of *Folly*'s satire, claiming that he 'could not keep from chuckling' when he read Dorp's suggestion 'that Erasmus could pacify those theologians whom the *Folly* upset if he would counter his praises of Folly with a praise of Wisdom', demonstrating that he had failed to understand the relationship between folly and wisdom that underpins Erasmus's text.[21]

More's 'Letter to a Monk' is a more exasperated and aggressive work. This is a response to another critique of *Folly* made by an anonymous English monk, now thought to be John Batmanson, a Carthusian based in London who was 'a quite active conservative polemicist'.[22] While the response to Dorp can be seen as Lucianic in nature, that to Batmanson is far more in line with More's later polemical writings in defence of the Church, a sign that the tables could be turned, as *Folly* recognized with its complicated responses to thinking, institutions and events. In his letter More argues that humanist approaches to theology are necessary for the survival and development of the Church and are not, as the monk argues, a Trojan horse that will shake its foundations. To rely on the deployment of dialectical logic to understand scripture and not to deploy the new tools made available to scholars since the Renaissance is to limit our understanding of God's word and, implicit in the argument, do the Devil's work for him.

More opens with a series of sarcastic rhetorical questions in response to the monk's argument that trusting in Erasmus is dangerous:

> How is it dangerous for me to believe that Erasmus has translated many New Testament passages better than the old translator, or for me to believe that Erasmus knows more about Greek and Latin literature than he did? Nor do I just believe it, I see it and know it for a fact; nor could anyone doubt it who has any command of both languages. How is it dangerous for me to enjoy reading those books which the most learned and most pious people are virtually unanimous in praising, and which the pope, best and

> gracious of primates, has twice now declared to be useful to scholars?[23]

The more languages one knows, the more one can read in various literatures and the more likely it is that one can be an accomplished and accurate translator. Therefore, it is foolish to think that Erasmus has not improved our understanding of the Bible, something that has been acknowledged by most important figures within the Church including the pope (More is referring to Leo X (in office 1513–21), with whom Erasmus had good relations, in stark contrast to his predecessor, Julius II (in office 1503–13), whom Erasmus imagined was refused entry into heaven in his satire *Julius Exclusus*). More declares that he feels sad that the monk cannot learn from Erasmus's many important volumes, and wonders whether a 'sly, crafty demon has managed to plant so much guile and insidious subterfuge in a heart as sincere and as candid' as the monk's.[24] This is another careful rhetorical attack, as More damns with faint praise, indicating that he thinks his opponent is gullible and stupid. In pointed contrast Erasmus would be far too astute to lapse into protracted false belief:

> How the truth never fails to assert itself! How contrivers of falsehoods are either exposed through some chance event, balked by the facts of the matter, or given away by their own indiscretion, like shrew-mice! For supposing Erasmus did have wrong opinions regarding the faith, how likely is it that he would be too stupid to see how dangerous this would be for him, and how likely is it that he would always be looking for people, or begging them even, to let him inform them in private that he was a heretic?[25]

The truth will always out, and it is inconceivable that Erasmus would be able to disguise his heretical beliefs should he want to, since he would be exposed eventually. More's point is that Erasmus is simply too intelligent to be a heretic, and such accusations, dangerous as they are, will inevitably fail. In stating that his opponent is making false assertions, More is turning the tables and suggesting that it is the monk who is more likely to be a heretic than Erasmus, through his failure to understand the nature of belief. More is being disingenuous, especially if one reads this passage against his later work as a hunter of heretics and his argument that it is extremely difficult to expose and catch heresy, which is always likely to spread if it is not stopped. In the 'Letter to Dorp', More acknowledges as much, in a telling passage. More suggests that heretics are 'either learned or unlearned', but is sceptical of Dorp's argument that debating theological matters with them will lead to a change of faith. The problem is especially acute when dealing with those conservative theologians who have deliberately avoided learning Greek and have stuck to the old methods, 'men who have never read any of the ancients or anything out of the scriptures except in the *Sentences* and their commentaries'.[26] They are the same as the authors who are taught in schools and whose thoughts they replicate. They cannot easily be used to combat heresy as they may well be heretics themselves and have

> dreamt up certain problems about God so ridiculous you might think they were raising a laugh and so blasphemous you might feel they were laughing directly at Him, they are certainly so zealous in raising objections to the faith and so backward in answering them that they seem to be in collusion with the opposition, defending the faith in jest and accepting it in earnest.[27]

Lucas Cranach the Elder, *Martin Luther*, 1528, oil on panel.

The section concludes with a fear that if the flammable material that is fuelling heresy is not removed then an enormous conflagration will surely consume the church:

> Now then, pitted against the sort of theologians I have mentioned, how soon are the heretics going to succumb, since they have been trained in the same school of tactics? Not very soon, to be sure, in my view, were they not more intimidated by one little bundle of faggots than by many large bundles of syllogisms.[28]

Here we have a passage that is definitely un-Erasmian in sentiment and points to the division between the two men: while Erasmus never wavered from his belief in persuasion and reason, More was prepared to defend the Church using whatever method was required to preserve the faith. Maarten van Dorp provides one form of threat to the Church; the monk, another – a conservative attack that may well undermine the efforts of the humanist modernizers. In the end it was the Protestant reformers whom More needed to silence. Indeed, a case can be made that it was the monk who was actually right, articulating the popular view that 'Erasmus laid the egg that Luther hatched.'[29]

More's comments in these defences of Erasmus were written just before Luther published his Ninety-Five Theses in Wittenberg (31 October 1517), triggering the Reformation. In 1515 no one could see what lay ahead and it was very unlikely that the conservative Henry VIII would do anything other than persecute Protestant heretics, which would help to explain why More provides Dorp with a more forceful threat than the monk – there was a far more obvious danger in Dorp's approach, one that could possibly reach More himself in England.

In his long letter More berates the monk for his pompous attack on Erasmus. He accuses him of appropriating the role of

God: 'You take as a basic assumption in this condemnation the thesis that Erasmus is utterly ignorant of scripture – just as you, I suppose, are omniscient.'[30] This is a further way of convicting the monk of heresy, as well as the deadly sin of pride. More accuses the monk of placing greater value on Church traditions than on understanding God's word: 'For who is idiotic enough to admit that he prizes his own ceremonies more than God's precepts when he knows that unless he abides by those precepts his own ceremonies are useless?'[31] Here, More sounds very like a Protestant critic of the Church, although he is not advocating the Protestant dictum of *sola scriptura*, but the belief that the Church has the right to determine and define the interpretation of the Bible through its wealth of learning and established traditions of exegesis. In an impassioned passage More distinguishes the virtuous Erasmus from his flawed and selfish critics, using the familiar rhetorical device of *occupatio*, denying that he is doing something he is doing and so drawing attention to his words:

> I have no intention of writing an encomium of Erasmus. For my own powers are unequal to so great a task, and everywhere on earth the best and most learned men are vying to do it as well as they possibly can. And even if they remained silent, his own rich benefactions to all mortal men, which commend him to virtuous men now, will commend him to all when his death puts an end to their envy . . . when at last he will be missed even by those people whose jaundiced, bleared eyes, as if dazzled with his intense brightness, cannot stand to look straight at him now . . . If anyone carefully considers the steady stream of massive, excellent, and numerous volumes that Erasmus has produced single-handedly, so many that you would think that one man would not even be equal to copying

> them all out, he will readily conclude that even if Erasmus were not totally preoccupied with virtue he would certainly have little time left to devote to vice.[32]

As Erasmus described More to von Hutten as a vision of human and scholarly perfection, so does More here represent Erasmus, a super-human man of virtue working harder than can be imagined to explain and defend the Church. Accordingly, it is unthinkable that such a committed, diligent and admirable man would have any desire or time to indulge in vice.

LETTERS

More and Erasmus's letters reveal much about their day-to-day lives and relationship, given how many were exchanged. The first surviving letter from More was written circa 17 February 1516, soon after the manuscript letters defending Erasmus were circulated. More writes about prominent churchmen and their prospective fortunes, and is confident that great things are in store for Erasmus very soon, possibly in England, because 'it is unnecessary to say what the attitude of the bishops is, and quite specially of his grace of Canterbury, and what a high opinion of you the king himself has.'[33] If a suitable benefice does not come his way, More suggests that the fault may lie in Erasmus himself 'for neglecting the objects of other men's ambition', a comment that neatly mirrors Erasmus's concerns about More being lost to political service. Erasmus's anxieties about money follow, a subject that was a constant theme of their correspondence, with More perhaps hinting at a frustration with his highly principled friend. The two had discussed Erasmus becoming a canon in Tournai (a French town under English jurisdiction), a role that Erasmus had turned down because he worried that his tenure would not last long, unless he could 'secure the approval of the other bishop [Louis Guillard]', who was at odds with his English counterparts in the town. Erasmus had seemed to be against taking the position when they discussed it in Bruges because he would have had to pay £10 in cash on taking up the benefice, and then pay off a mortgage on the house that came with it. Now he seems in favour, but More explains that the role has since gone to another candidate. However, he adds, Cardinal Wolsey, who oversees such ecclesiastical offices, owes Erasmus 'a richer one', and Wolsey 'often threw in a friendly mention of you' when More met him.[34] More's long discussion of the issue suggests that, as much as he sympathized with his friend's predicament, he found Erasmus's vacillating and unmovable desire to preserve his independence somewhat trying. More discusses the position of envoy, one he had taken for a recent diplomatic visit to Flanders, stating rather pointedly that he has never much liked the role, 'Nor does it seem to me so suitable for us laymen as it is for you priests, who to begin with have no wives and children at home.'[35]

Much of the correspondence, as might be expected, concerns their writings. More often solicits, perhaps slightly nervously, Erasmus's opinions of his work. In a letter of circa 26 June 1516 More asks Erasmus before he signs off, 'What think you of my letter to Dorp? I very much want to know,' which suggests an understandable anxiety, possibly because of the comments on heresy.[36] Later that year More sent Erasmus *Utopia*: 'I send you my book on Nowhere, and you will find it is nowhere well written.' More urged that Erasmus 'must do what [he] can for it' to ensure its publication. Again, More expresses his anxiety and hopes for the older man's approval, which will give him the confidence that the work will be well received once it is in the public domain. If it can please Erasmus, then surely it will satisfy all the readers he might care about. A letter of 15 December 1516, after Erasmus expressed his regard for More's fiction, confirms this sense of eager anticipation and More's hope that *Utopia* will get a favourable reception when it is published, an imminent event: 'As for my *Utopia*, your letter gave me hope, on which I batten greedily, and I now expect it daily with the feelings of a mother expecting her son's return from foreign parts.'[37] He had expressed a similar feeling of nervous excitement when describing a letter he received from Cuthbert Tunstall a few days earlier, which he describes to Erasmus in his letter of circa 4 December 1516:

> I had a letter the other day from Tunstall, full of the most friendly feeling; I promise you, his opinion of my republic, so frank and so favourable, cheered me more, dearest Erasmus, than a nugget of pure gold. So you can't think how I now fancy myself; I have grown taller, I hold my head higher, for I have continually before my eyes the perpetual office of prince which my Utopians are planning to confer on me. In fact I see myself already crowned with that distinguished diadem of corn-ears, a splendid sight in my Franciscan robe, bearing that venerable sceptre consisting of a sheaf of corn, and accompanied by a distinguished company of citizens of Amaurote [the capital of Utopia].[38]

The joke, one of many that they share in the letters, highlights the boyish delight that More demonstrates to Erasmus as a token of his friendly esteem and a sign of their intimate relationship.

Another favourite subject is the peril of travel, expressed more often by Erasmus than More, an indication of his anxieties as he aged. Writing on 30 May 1517 from Antwerp, Erasmus describes a perilous Channel crossing, exacerbated by terrible weather bringing with it disease to the coastal areas of England and France:

> On the first of May, with the wind increasing and by now actually against us, in the middle of the night I was roughly put ashore from a ship's boat not without peril under some cliffs on the French coast not far from Boulogne. The wind soon became very rough, and for the rest of our journey was made worse by our being so near the coast. It has caused many deaths in these parts from inflammation of the throat and lungs, and still does.[39]

Channel crossings were often fraught and dangerous at this time, so Erasmus was not exaggerating his legitimate fear.[40] Admitting his nervousness to More, just as More revealed his anxieties about his books, was a sign of their mutual regard and ability to speak honestly in ways they might have avoided with other people. Erasmus and More lived out their friendship in private and in public, a close relationship between two intellectual giants that shaped not just their writing and their careers, but also the nature of life and thought in sixteenth-century Europe. In a letter to Erasmus from Calais (5 November 1517), inspired by some derogatory comments by a friar, More composed an epigram about their friendship, declaring it far more significant and substantial than that of monks, brothers in religion:

> Quoth I, of two great friends in brief
> The affection to declare,
> 'Such friends they are as once of old
> Castor and Pollux were.'
> An owlish brother takes me up,
> Of those who wear the cowl:
> 'Who friends and brothers thus confounds,
> Sure, he must be an owl!'
> 'How so? What can more friendly be
> Than brother is to brother?'

He laughed at one who did not know
What's known to every other;
'A large and crowded house is ours,
Brothers ten score may be;
In those ten score (my life upon't)
Two friends you will not see.'[41]

ORBIS TYPVS VNIVERSALIS IVXTA HYDROGRAPHORVM TRADITIONEM
OCEANVS OCCIDENTALIS
ASIA
AFRICA
AMERICA
MARE INDICVM

THREE

Utopia

The 'little book' known to history as *Utopia* is – intentionally – a mystery wrapped in an enigma, all packaged as a riddle. This is indicated by the name of More's imagined island, Utopia, which can mean both 'best place' (*eutopia*) and 'no place' (*outopia*). Everything about More's best-known work is puzzling as he plays with notions of reality and fantasy, and authorship and authority. In some ways, this is the point. If nothing else, *Utopia* asks the reader to question what is 'real' about the world they live in and, as a consequence, what really matters. Money, property and social standing are pernicious fictions, as make-believe as More's little island, and yet they determine everything about his contemporary Britain. In Utopia, the citizens value what is real and enduring – reason, virtue and community – all of which are eroded in Britain. So which island is more fantastical?

HYTHLODAY'S COUNSEL

Utopia was first published in Leuven in 1516, with a definitive edition produced two years later in Basel.[1] It appears in two parts (books), and it has long been accepted in the scholarship that these were composed in reverse order.[2] Book Two was almost certainly written over the summer of 1515, while More was on the diplomatic mission to the Low Countries that he describes

World map by Martin Waldseemüller, 1513, woodcut.

in the opening of Book One (the same period during which he wrote his 'Letter to Dorp'). During a pause in negotiations, he travelled to see Pieter Gillis in Antwerp and seems to have returned to England in October with Book Two – the description of the island – in his travel bags. It was on returning to London, with all its competing demands and busyness, that More wrote Book One and the close of Book Two, an enigmatic framing for the mysterious island.

It opens in the reality of More's day. More is on a diplomatic mission to the Low Countries on behalf of his king, Henry VIII. Waiting on his counterparts to return with orders from their prince, More travels from Bruges to Antwerp, and stays with Gillis. The break in reality comes as More leaves the central church in Antwerp and Gillis introduces him to a man called Raphael Hythloday.[3] Hythloday is not a historical figure, though More writes him as a former shipmate of the real-world Amerigo Vespucci, who had died three years before.

Hythloday is an explorer, sailor and scholar, especially versed in More's much-esteemed classical Greek. Hythloday's arrival in the text alerts the reader to the many Greek-language puns and riddles scattered throughout, as well as More's intended obfuscation of his central argument. The man's first name, Raphael, recalls the archangel of the same name, known for guiding lost travellers and healing blindness – clear signs that he might be the authority in the discussion that follows. His last name, however, poses problems, as More intended it to. In the Greek, *hythlos* means 'nonsense' or 'idle talk'. The second half of his name could come from *daois* meaning 'destructive' or *hodaois* meaning 'merchant' or 'peddler'.[4] Was Raphael the destroyer of idle talk or the peddler of nonsense? Or both?

Hythloday becomes the central interlocutor to the bulk of Book One, known in the scholarship as the 'dialogue of counsel', which takes place between him and the narrator of Book One:

More himself. The reader might be forgiven for assuming, then, that it is More with whom they ought to side in the discussion, but once again *Utopia* is not nearly so straightforward. The character of More is better identified as 'Morus' (as he appears in the original Latin text), which provides a quibble on 'mulberry' (*Morus*), the tree well known as that of the 'wise fool', as he is not necessarily the literal persona of the author.[5] Most readers of *Utopia* would know that 'Morus' could mean 'folly' or 'fool', thanks to Erasmus's *Praise of Folly*. Let the games begin, More signals.

The dialogue itself takes as its central question one often tackled by the classical thinkers so admired by More (and Hythloday) and revived by his contemporaries: what was the best life? There tended to be three possible answers. The first, especially touted by the Greek philosophers admired by Hythloday, such as Plato, was the 'contemplative life': a life of quiet isolation and the contemplation of philosophical truths. The second, a favourite of Roman writers such as Cicero, was the 'active life', a life dedicated

Pieter Aertsen, *Christ in the House of Martha and Mary*, 1553, oil on panel.

to the service of the commonwealth, even if that meant occasionally compromising those exalted truths. Finally, many thinkers, including Church Fathers whom More himself admired, such as St Augustine and St Chrysostom, advocated for the 'mixed life', which involved combining a monkish devotion to God and divine truth with a life of busyness, pursuing virtuous ends in the world of business and politics.[6] Plato would have called such a pursuit impossible.

Thus does his follower, Hythloday. The dialogue begins when Gillis (who initiates the dialogue, but then quickly disappears from it) declares to Hythloday, 'I wonder that you do not attach yourself to some king.' For then, 'you would not only serve your own interests excellently, but be of great assistance in the advancement of all your relatives and friends.'[7] Gillis places the dutiful call to the active life in the context of his contemporary Europe, one not of republics, but of kings. In such a context, the best position available to the active, learned citizen was that of a counsellor to a king. And this is how Morus reframes the question:

> It seems to me you will do what is worthy of you and of this generous and truly philosophic spirit of yours if you so order your life as to apply your talent and industry to the public interest, even if it involves some personal disadvantages to yourself. This you can never do with as great profit as if you are a councillor to some great monarch.[8]

Morus takes the Ciceronian position, advocating the 'active life'; Hythloday responds as Plato would, suggesting that the 'contemplative life' is the only morally defensible choice.

Woven into their dialogue on the best life are other critiques and allusions, though always with a central theme of the conflict between private and public good. Hythloday launches into a long tale about a visit to the home of John Morton (where More had spent some of his childhood), in which he critiques England's laws, especially those around capital punishment for thieves, which leads onto a discussion about the injustices of enclosure of common land. His point is that no one listens to his counsel (an argument undermined by his telling of it), but along the way More has smuggled in some biting social commentary, along with some entertaining witticisms. Likewise, Hythloday describes an imagined council to the king of France, as councillors compete to suggest ways in which the king might fill his coffers (many of which are reminiscent of those used in the reign of Henry VII) in order to fund foreign wars and conquests. More is able to use this lengthy example to launch critiques of kings real and imagined, past and present, as well as their councillors, while the point remains about the (in)viability of Hythloday's counsel. Hythloday concludes, 'if I tried to obtrude these and like ideas on men strongly inclined to the opposite way of thinking, to what deaf ears should I tell the tale!'[9]

Morus is only too happy to agree, 'Deaf indeed, without doubt.' In contrast to this 'academic philosophy which thinks that everything is suitable to every place', Morus suggests a more civil philosophy, which 'knows its stage, adapts itself to the play in hand, and performs its role nearly and appropriately'.[10] Using the metaphor of the stage-play which he had developed in his earlier works, More has Morus advocate for a sort of counsel which does not interrupt the play at hand. Instead, he advises that 'Whatever play is being performed, perform it as best you can and do not upset it all simply because you think of another which has more interest.' It is a position of compromise, for 'What you cannot turn to good you must at least make as little bad as you can.' As Morus asserts, perfect action requires perfect men, 'a situation which I do not expect for a great many years to come!', an early allusion to the paradox of Utopia, which will be played out in Book Two.[11]

Hythloday responds in typically Platonic terms: to do this will only be to pollute oneself with others' vices and achieve nothing in the pursuit of virtue. Hythloday is uncompromising because, he says, the court is uncompromising. 'At court there is no room for dissembling, nor may one shut one's eyes to things. One must openly approve the worst counsel and subscribe to the most ruinous decrees. He would be counted a spy and a traitor, who gives only faint praise to evil counsels.'[12] He uses an example from Plato's *Republic* to demonstrate his point:

> For this reason, Plato by a very fine comparison shows why philosophers are right in abstaining from administration of the commonwealth. They observe the people rushing out into the streets and being soaked by constant showers and cannot induce them to go indoors and escape the rain. They know that, if they go out, they can do no good but will only get wet with the rest. Therefore, being content if they themselves are at least safe, they keep at home, since they cannot remedy the folly of others.[13]

Interestingly, More's later life provides three other interpretations of this 'comparison'. The first comes in a letter he received from his stepdaughter, Alice Allington, who attributes it to More's successor in the Chancellorship, Thomas Audley. Audley, according to Allington, mockingly compared the imprisoned More to a wise man in a country of fools who remains inside for fear of the rain only to miss out on the establishment of a government, now ruled by fools instead of the wise, an interpretation like one that the fictional Morus might have made. More responds by suggesting that this tale had often been used by Cardinal Wolsey in the king's council, who employed it as justification for England's engagement in the wars between France and Spain, much like the king's council described by Hythloday. More, however, then provides another way of thinking about the story, one at odds with those of Hythloday, Audley and Wolsey. Any desire on the part of the wise to rule the fools in the rain in fact made them foolish, and they were foolish even before the rains arrived. Men ought to learn to rule themselves first, and then neither rain nor rulership will matter.[14]

In *Utopia*, Hythloday uses this discussion to transition smoothly into a discussion of the lack of private property in Utopia, for 'I am fully persuaded that no just and even distribution of goods can be made and that no happiness can be found in human affairs unless private property is utterly abolished.'[15] In other words, Hythloday will continue to withhold his counsel from the courts of princes until there is a utopian scenario, which allows More to hand the narration over to Hythloday in Book Two.

MORE AND MORUS

Alongside Book One, it is probable that More also wrote the closing paragraphs of *Utopia* in those busy months in London, framing his tale of the fantastical island which lacks the artificialities that plague the real world. The narration returns to Morus, who reflects on what Hythloday has told them. Many of the institutions of the Utopians, including their way of waging war, their religious practices and beliefs and most of all their communal property, he concludes, are 'absurd'. It is this last, he reckons, which 'utterly overthrows all the nobility, magnificence, splendour, and majesty which are, in the estimation of the common people, the true glories and ornaments of the commonwealth'.[16] Of course, this judgement must be read with an eye to More's love for irony. The Utopians' common property undermines European notions of nobility and majesty and removes the 'adornments' of contemporary commonwealths; the question is whether or not More would have endorsed this unadornment. Both More and Erasmus agreed that the elaborate costuming of monarchs, for instance, was only valuable if the various accessories – crown, sceptre, robe and so on – acted as reminders of associated virtues. *Utopia* itself has often been read as an argument for *vera nobilitas* (true nobility), the idea that virtue comes from character, not birth and wealth.[17] If this is Morus's sole objection, then, it would not be persuasive to any contemporary humanist reader. More ends the book with a final thought from Morus:

> Meanwhile, though in other respects he [Hythloday] is a man of the most undoubted learning as well of the greatest knowledge of human affairs, I cannot agree with all that he said. But I readily admit that there are very many features in the Utopian commonwealth which it is easier for me to wish for in our countries than to have any hope of seeing realized.[18]

The sentiment seems to reflect Morus's arguments about counsel: not expecting to see that all men are good for many years to come (a dry dismissal of the idea that it could happen at all). Reading these final comments in the context of More's wider oeuvre, we are also offered insights similar to those provided in the interpretation of Plato's rain-shy wise men. More uses a similar phrase (this time in English, rather than *Utopia*'s Latin) in his *Apology*, nearly two decades later.

> And therefore, good Christian readers, would God the world were such as every man were so good – spiritual, temporal, and all – that neither party could find any fault in other, and all these heretics so clean gone and forgotten, and all those that are infected were so clean turned and changed that no man needed either abjuration or punishment. But since that this is *more easy to wish than likely to*

> *look for*, therefore is it wisdom that spiritual and temporal both, albeit men be not all saints, yet if their conditions be tolerable, either party labor to make himself better, and charitably somewhat either party bear with other.[19]

The discussion here is not unlike that in *Utopia* – how do we act in an imperfect world of imperfect men? – but is presented in the context of prideful heresy, rather than the prideful greed that is the focus of *Utopia*. Here, the lesson is made more explicit; the reader is advised to work on themself first, just as More concludes in regard to Plato's rainy tale. It is an unsatisfying answer to the deep humanist questions that *Utopia* tackles, which is perhaps why More does not provide it there. Instead, the reader is left to ponder the question of how they might lead the best life in the context of a corrupted world – whether in the isolated contemplation of truth or the vicious and pernicious princely court, alone.

UTOPIAN LESSONS

If, as seems likely, Book Two of *Utopia* was written before Book One, then we get a sense that More was not confident that, on its own, his representation of a remote island people would be read as he wanted it to be. Indeed, ever since the book was published critics have been arguing about More's intentions, how they might be recovered and understood, and how we should understand the Utopians and their social and religious practices. There are, however, some passages that would seem to provide evidence of More's intentions, notably Raphael's description of the Utopians' treatment of disease and death:

> The sick . . . are very lovingly cared for, nothing being omitted which may restore them to health, whether in the way of medicine or diet. They console the incurably

> diseased by sitting and conversing with them and by applying all possible alleviations. But if a disease is not only incurable but also distressing and agonizing without any cessation, then the priests and the public officials exhort the man, since he is now unequal to all life's duties, a burden to himself, and a trouble to others, and is living beyond the time of his death, to make up his mind not to foster the pest and plague any longer nor to hesitate to die now that life is torture to him but, relying on good hope, to free himself from this bitter life as from prison and the rack, or else voluntarily to permit others to free him. In this course he will act wisely since by death he will put an end not to enjoyment but to torture. Because in doing so he will be obeying the counsels of the priests, who are God's interpreters, it will be a pious and holy action.[20]

The passage resembles more recent debates on euthanasia and assisted dying and so has a superficial plausibility, at least for present-day readers. The desire to alleviate a person wracked with pain and end pointless suffering seems entirely reasonable, so it is no wonder that the rational Utopians practise euthanasia when all hope of productive life has gone. The suffering of those dying can seem like being trapped inside a body that is a prison, and surely no one really wants to endure pestilence, the plague or the rack if they can avoid them. Accordingly, the priests and government officials who act to end a life when it is necessary are doing God's work and are seen as His agents.

However, it is unlikely that More expected his readers to take this passage at face value. A man who soon afterwards confronted those he saw as heretics with a defence of the Church and its duty to defend the right of the individual soul in *The Supplication of Souls* could not support the notion that humans could take the decision, rational enough in its way, to end life simply to ease suffering.

Perhaps, even, a case could be made that someone prepared to argue that heretics should be burned to death in order not only to save their souls but to purify the land from those who would infect it with false belief – and thus imperil others' souls – was unlikely to see prison and the most brutal instrument of torture, the rack, as simply modes of reducing the purposeful enjoyment of life.

The passage is perhaps best read as a comment on Christian revelation. If the Bible and the life of Christ had not outlined God's plan for mankind's salvation, then the Utopians' view would be sensible and reasonable, making them very like the virtuous pagans rescued by Christ in the Harrowing of Hell, in the period between his death and resurrection, according to orthodox Church doctrine and referred to in More's 'Letter to Bugenhagen'.[21] Therefore, it would be reasonable to think about ending life voluntarily, if the scriptures had not prohibited such a practice because of the inviolable nature of the soul and the injunction against suicide as the destruction of God's gift of life to humankind and a failure to accept his plan for us. In the *Dialogue Concerning Heresies*, More argued that Richard Hunne (d. 1514), a wealthy merchant tailor and critic of the Church who was influenced by the Lollards, the late medieval movement often seen as proto-Protestant, had killed himself in prison.[22] Hunne's case was notorious: he refused to pay mortuary fees to the Church after the death of his infant son, was subsequently excommunicated and was then imprisoned for heresy when a Wycliffe Bible, the earliest translation into English, was discovered in his house. When he was found hanged in his cell the clergy defended the Church and argued that Hunne's death was suicide; but a coroner's court found that he had been tortured and then murdered, leaving as a mystery the death of a figure who was seen as a heretic by Catholics and a martyr by Protestants. Given More's argument that a heretic had killed himself 'for weariness of his life' and so was prepared to suffer a 'shameful death', it is implausible that the Utopians' logic is one that More supported.[23]

More's argument throughout his writings on religion is that neither the scriptures on their own nor fallible human reason on its own can be trusted as a guide to understanding the mysteries of the faith and God's plan. Rather, reason and revelation must be taken together, the Bible always showing itself to be in line with reason if read properly (that is, by the officers of the Church). Humankind has free will and the ability to exercise the right choices, a point made repeatedly in *The Confutation of Tyndale's Answer*.[24]

Elsewhere in the description of the Utopians' customs, we have to decide how to read what they do, as More challenges his readers to read his book carefully and properly (which is why Book One was so important as a guide). When choosing spouses the Utopians

> seriously and strictly espouse a custom which seemed to us very foolish and extremely ridiculous. The woman, whether maiden or widow, is shown naked to the suitor by a worthy and respectable matron, and similarly the suitor is presented naked before the maiden by a discreet man. We laughed at this custom and condemned it as foolish. They, on the other hand, marvelled at the remarkable folly of all other nations.[25]

Are the Europeans right to poke fun at the Utopians? Or are the Utopians justified in thinking that other countries are so foolish not to want to see their prospective life partner naked before deciding to marry them? The Utopians argue that no one would buy a horse without checking it over properly, and so it should be the same with a wife or husband. In this example the stakes would seem to be relatively low, the difference between the two cultures a contrast of logic and custom with, surely, the Utopians' logic shown to be rather too humiliating for people and not considering the extent of normal human emotions. Life cannot always be quite so rationally conceived. The same might be said about the Utopians' attitude to divorce, which is permitted when one party commits adultery or demonstrates 'intolerable offensiveness of disposition'.[26] Again, there is a logic here but one that More surely did not support as a valid practice for sixteenth-century England, where marriage was a sacrament involving a promise of fidelity between two people.

In other places we cannot be sure exactly what More thinks, but it is more likely that he thought the Utopian example had much to teach Europeans. The Utopians cannot tolerate laziness, and so they establish rules to ensure that everyone always undertakes some productive labour for the worker's own benefit and for that of the whole community. Accordingly, a class of officials have been established, the syphogrants, whose only function is 'to manage and provide that no one sit idle, but that each apply himself industriously to his trade', but within the bounds of reason so that no one is 'wearied like a beast of burden with constant toil from early morning till late at night'.[27] Utopian thought is based on pleasure, very like the ancient Greek philosophy of Epicureanism, which stipulated that life should be based on regulation and moderation, steering between extremes to ensure the maximization of pleasure and minimization of pain. Raphael lambasts European society with its concentration on magnificence and excess, arguing that if all those 'busied with unprofitable crafts, as well as all the lazy and idle throng' were employed in useful work, 'You can easily see how small an allowance of time would be enough and to spare for the production of all that is required by necessity or comfort (or even pleasure, provided it be genuine and natural).'[28] Later we learn that the Utopians enjoy lengthy collective suppers at which music is played, spices burnt and perfumes scattered: 'For they are somewhat too much inclined to this attitude of mind: that no kind of pleasure is forbidden, provided no harm comes of it.'[29] The Utopian logic is evident, and their attitude is hard to fault when seen in isolation and taken on its own terms. However, Raphael's muted admonishment is surely endorsed by More, indicating that the Utopians care too much about the balance of pleasure and pain, and do not have enough capacity to think about spiritual matters.

We might also be sceptical about the Utopians' attitude to colonization, articulated just at the time that European colonization was becoming more feasible and widespread as the Spanish started to occupy large swathes of South America, and the English crown was provided with offers by intrepid mariners that it refused. The Utopians' attitude to colonization is indeed logical:

> And if the population throughout the island should happen to swell above fixed quotas, they enroll citizens out of every city and, on the mainland nearest them, wherever the natives have much unoccupied and uncultivated land, they found a colony under their own laws. They join with themselves the natives if they are willing to dwell with them. When such a union takes place, the two parties gradually and easily merge and together absorb the same way of life and the same customs, much to the great advantage of both peoples. By their procedures they make the land sufficient for both, which previously seemed poor and barren to the natives. The inhabitants who refuse to live according to their laws, they drive from the territory which they carve out for themselves. If they resist, they wage war against them. They consider it a most just cause for war when a people which does not use its soil but keeps it idle and waste nevertheless forbids the use and possession of it to others who by the rule of nature ought to be maintained by it.[30]

The passage is unsettling for a reader with its mixture of practical, sensible and rational solutions mingled with shocking brutality. 'Waste' is a key concept throughout the book, Raphael admiring the ways in which the Utopians are always productive and active, working towards the betterment of the commonwealth and the interest of its citizens. Idleness cannot be tolerated, and Raphael openly supports the work ethic of the Utopians who are 'neither idle nor busied with useless occupations', making 'it easy to calculate how much good work can be produced in a very few hours'.[31] The same logic can be applied to land, which must not lie 'waste' and be used unproductively, as happens in the famous description of sheep farming in contemporary England in Book One, whereby unscrupulous landowners make huge profits for themselves and impoverish the people by enclosing vast tracts of land on which their monstrous herds of sheep can graze, ensuring a reduction in crops and food for the common people. The Utopians' policy of colonization follows logically from this assumption that land and labour need to be regulated properly so that the best use of resources is ensured, and the people can be fed. Indeed, the Utopians' assumptions are in line with contemporary thinking about land use and colonization, and it was a staple of European thinking that if a people could not use their land effectively, then colonial settlers had the right to take over and ensure that it was used better.[32]

Read one way the Utopians' policy of colonial expansion might seem entirely reasonable and simply working towards the common good. We might, however, wonder whether the use of the idea of a 'just war' against those who are not persuaded to join the Utopians and support their domination is entirely appropriate. Theories of 'just war' had been extensively debated throughout the European Middle Ages and early Renaissance, with many questioning whether those who claimed they were fighting 'just wars' were being honest.[33] A year after *Utopia* appeared Erasmus published his famous anti-war polemic, *Dulce bellum inexpertis* (published in the *Adages* in 1515, separately in 1517). Erasmus was not a pacifist and supported the prospect of a crusade against the Ottoman Empire, but he was sceptical of the justifications for warfare employed within Europe, especially by the papacy within the Italian peninsula. Erasmus had published the satirical dialogue *Julius Exclusus* in 1514, which represented the recently deceased 'warrior Pope', Julius II, denied his place in heaven for his wicked deeds in waging destructive war simply for his personal glory.

Is More via Raphael encouraging readers to see the Utopians as similarly bellicose? It is extremely hard to tell. The Utopians do use land productively and their policies are clearly designed for the benefit of everyone living off the land, but only if the people accept the right of the Utopians to dominate and control them. *Utopia* is a work that reads like travel or colonial writing, Raphael's journey to the imagined island combining Plato's theories of ideal government with contemporary travelogues of voyagers who had crossed the Atlantic to the 'New World' (although there are also hints that it may be located somewhere in the Indian Ocean).[34] Here, it is the Utopians who are the colonizers, acting like Europeans taking over another people, which forces European readers to think about what it is they have done and what they want to do in the future. When *Utopia* was published, England was not a colonial power (apart from its occupation of Ireland) and had a relatively lowly status within Europe. However, it was connected to the major European superpower and colonial force, Spain, through the marriage of Henry VIII and Catherine of Aragon (11 June 1509). Catherine was the daughter of Ferdinand and Isabella, the Catholic rulers who had united Spain and expelled the Moorish rulers of the South.

In fact the 'Reconquest' took place when the last stronghold, Granada, surrendered in 1492, enabling the Castilian monarchs to forcibly convert or expel the Muslims and Jews who had lived in Al-Andalus. In the same year, Columbus, working for Ferdinand and Isabella, reached the Americas, reporting on his achievement in 1493. Therefore, via the marriage, England was, if not a colonial power, then closely joined to the heart of European colonialism. Even so, Henry VIII, his mind on success in European wars, most obviously in France, seemed indifferent to appeals for support for transatlantic voyages. Certainly, he was less keen than his father, Henry VII, although he did employ a Venetian, Sebastian Cabot (*c*. 1481/2–1557), who had sailed to find the Northwest Passage during the previous reign, as a cartographer.

In representing the Utopians as a colonial power, More was asking his readers to think about the implications of colonial ventures and whether colonialism could be justified. Notably absent, of course, is the issue of religion. The principal justification for the Spanish conquest of South America was the need to save the souls of the pagan native inhabitants by converting them to Catholicism.[35] For the Utopians, the issue is efficient land usage, a pressing problem as the first book of *Utopia* argues, but surely not of the same order. Readers are forced to wonder whether the crusading 'just wars' that the Utopians fight are actually justifiable.

The same questions are raised by the Utopians' practice of slavery, in a section that owes much to More's thinking about ancient Greece and the slavery practised in Athens and other Greek states.[36] There are various levels of slavery in Utopia:

> Prisoners of war are not enslaved unless captured in wars fought by the Utopians themselves; nor are the sons of slaves, nor anyone who was in slavery when acquired from some foreign country. Their slaves are either such as are enslaved in their own country for heinous crimes or such as have been condemned to death elsewhere for some offence. The greater number are of this latter kind. They carry away many of them; sometimes they buy them

cheaply; but often they ask for them and get them for nothing. These classes of slaves they keep not only continually at work but also in chains. Their own countrymen are dealt with more harshly, since their conduct is regarded as all the more regrettable and deserving a more severe

Raphael, *Pope Julius II*, 1511, oil on poplar panel.

> punishment as an object lesson because, having had an excellent rearing to a virtuous life, they still could not be restrained from crime.[37]

The passage asks readers about the purpose of slavery; whether it is permissible or reasonable; and, if so, what might be its benefits and disadvantages. The passage has to be read, yet again, against the background of absent Christianity. In Spain, there were public debates about the nature of the Native Americans and whether they were the 'natural slaves' described by Aristotle. These were people who could never be fully human and who were consigned to a life of simple drudgery, making the lives of their superiors better in return for the provision of their own basic needs. Others argued that this perception was quite wrong and that the Spanish had a duty to convert the Native Americans,

Spanish school, *Isabella I* and *Ferdinand II*, 15th century, oil on panel.

who when exposed to the truth of Christianity would become Christians themselves.

The Utopians' attitude to slavery might well seem entirely rational. They enslave those they capture in war, but the children of those slaves are not themselves born into servitude, so slavery is considered a condition that lasts for life but is not then inherited. Furthermore, the Utopians are more merciful than other countries, enslaving those who would have been executed elsewhere, and so they often acquire prisoners as slaves as a result. These slaves work for the Utopians and carry the signs of their stigmatized condition (chains). There is, in effect, very little difference between slaves and prisoners. In marked contrast is the treatment of transgressive Utopians, who are seen as far more culpable, since they should know better than to undermine the society that has nurtured them so well.

It is an indication of the desirable nature of Utopian society – at least, as seen by the enthusiastic Raphael – that many volunteer to become slaves:

> There is yet another class of slaves, for sometimes a hard-working and poverty-stricken drudge of another country voluntarily chooses slavery in Utopia. These individuals are well treated and, except that they have a little more work assigned to them as being used to it, are dealt with almost as leniently as citizens. If anyone wishes to depart, which seldom happens, they do not detain him against his will nor send him away empty-handed.[38]

The passage suggests that More is not thinking about slavery as we understand it, the chattel slavery whereby one person had ownership of another. Such slavery was the cornerstone of the European Atlantic slave trade, which was taking place in the Iberian peninsula while More was alive, and which transformed the British economy in the seventeenth century. Here, we witness a mixture of work practices, Utopian society being so advanced that even the lowest subjects enjoy a higher standard of living than those in neighbouring societies, so that they voluntarily enslave themselves out of rational self-interest. More's further implication may well be that slavery is at odds with Christianity, or, at least, Christians should not enslave other Christians (enslaving pagans and those who refuse to be enlightened may be acceptable). In the ancient world such brutal practices may well have made sense and followed a logic, but in Christendom they work, if they work at all, as part of a penal system.

Raphael takes great pains to describe Utopian religious beliefs and practices. These vary from region to region, with some worshiping the sun, others the moon, and others one of the planets. However, they all agree that there is a supreme being 'to whom are due both the creation and the providential government of the world'.[39] The differences between modes of belief are gradually diminishing, and 'they are all beginning to depart from this medley of superstitions and are coming to unite in that one religion which seems to surpass the rest in reasonableness.'[40] In other words, the Utopians are starting to realize that Christianity is the one, rational form of belief that explains the nature of the supreme being, God. In this readiness to be converted and the closeness of their religion to Christianity, the Utopians are like the good, docile natives that Europeans encountered in the Americas. And, in a fantasy of European belief in progress, Raphael can report that this conversion is indeed what is happening:

> But after they had heard from us the name of Christ, His teaching, His character, His miracles, and the no less wonderful constancy of the many martyrs whose blood freely shed had drawn so many nations far and wide into their fellowship, you would not believe how readily disposed

> they, too, were to join it, whether through the rather mysterious inspiration of God or because they thought it nearest to that belief which has the widest prevalence among them. But I think that this factor, too, was of no small weight, that they had heard that His disciples' common way of life had been pleasing to Christ and that it is still in use among the truest societies of Christians. But whatever it was that influenced them, not a few joined our religion and were cleansed by the holy water of baptism.[41]

The Utopians realize that Christianity, which in 1516 was still a united religion in advance of the schism ignited by Luther's Theses of 1517, is the most reasonable form of religion. Not only does it explain God's authority and His plan for the peoples of the world, but it has a supporting history and series of traditions that validate the form that it takes. There are miracles, which make sense when the overall design of the world is outlined, and martyrs whose deaths have helped the Church to spread and secure more converts. Reason and mystery are not just compatible in *Utopia*: they are mutually reinforcing. What Raphael explains and the Utopians accept is squarely in line with More's defences of the Church in his writings against heresy.

As a detail that seems like a supplement, but which is a clue to More's designs in his fiction, the Utopians are inspired by the 'common way' of life that Christ's disciples enjoy. How this manifests itself is not made clear, but, as well as the significance of holding property in common as early Christians did, More could also be referring to monasteries; or perhaps congregations at worship; or even the simple equality of Christians through shared ways of living. The point is that the Utopians' way of thinking has much in common with Christianity – at least, as envisaged by More. Both seek to find connections and to develop what binds people together to form a community of like-minded believers, and both are hostile to individuals who refuse to fit in and believe they know better than long-established traditions: in essence, the case that More made against Protestantism. The Utopians' way of life is imagined to make Christian readers think about what it is that makes them Christians and to wonder whether they might follow Christian practices a bit better. One way, following the Utopians, is to see how a shared, common life might be improved.

PARATEXTS

When we speak of *Utopia* as a published text, we cannot speak of its two books alone. More's tale was packaged (perhaps with his knowledge, probably by his friends and collaborators in the European Republic of Letters) in a series of other materials – both textual and visual – known as 'paratexts', all of which enhance (or further obscure) our understanding of the central text, and especially its mutable relationship with reality.[42] Though it was typical for a text to enter the world with a dedication and perhaps a poem or two to the brilliance of the author or their topic, *Utopia* was clothed in far greater and grander paratextual material than most other books of its age.

As More told Erasmus, who was handling the publication of *Utopia*, 'I am most anxious to have it published soon and also that it be handsomely set off with the highest of recommendations, if possible, from several people, both intellectuals and distinguished statesmen.'[43] This, the well-connected Erasmus was able to provide. By the time of the definitive 1518 Basel edition, *Utopia* was prefaced with letters from Erasmus to the printer Johannes Froben; a letter from Guillaume Budé to Thomas Lupset – two of Europe's leading humanists; a letter from Pieter Gillis to Hieronymus van Busleyden, another European intellectual light and political figure; and the letter of More to Gillis, which most clearly sets the scene for what follows.[44] Following the text are more letters, from Busleyden to More, and then verses from two German humanists, Gerard Geldenhouwer and Cornelius Schrijver.

These letters and poems combine praise for More with musings about the text itself. Erasmus's letter to Froben contains some of the biographical information also present in his letter to von Hutten, about More's poetical inclination as a 'mere youth' and, echoing More's letter to Gillis, his many commitments:

> Not only is he married, not only has he family cares to attend to, not only does he hold a public office and handle an overwhelming number of legal cases, but he is distracted by so many and weighty affairs of the realm that you wonder he finds time even to think of books.[45]

Budé's letter waxes long about the merits of Utopian principles, summarizing them for the reader:

> (1) the equality of all things, good and bad, among fellow-citizens or, if you prefer, their civic sharing of them, absolute on all counts; (2) the resolute and tenacious love of peace and quiet; and (3) the contempt of gold and silver. These are the three overthrowers, I may say, of all frauds, impostures, swindles, rogueries, and wicked deceptions.[46]

His letter adds to the believable fiction of the entire enterprise, by musing on the possible location of this – as he calls it – 'never-land'.[47] Gillis, likewise, adds his testimony to the veracity of what follows, noting to Busleyden that he 'heard Raphael Hythloday's own words sounding in my ears'.[48] He provides a lively reason for why the location of the island remains unknown:

> While Raphael was speaking on the topic, one of More's servants had come up to him to whisper something or other in his ear. I was therefore listening all the more intently when one of our company who had, I suppose, caught cold on shipboard, coughed so loudly that I lost some phrases of what Raphael said. I shall not rest, however, till I have full information on this point so that I shall be able to tell you exactly not only the location of the island but even the longitude and latitude – provided that our friend Hythloday be alive and safe.[49]

More's own letter to Gillis continues this fiction, though in More's account 'We forgot to ask, and he forgot to say, in what part of the new world Utopia lies,' and so he asks Gillis to follow up with Hythloday, when he next sees him.[50]

Interspersed among these letters from flesh-and-blood individuals of the humanist Republic of Letters are Utopian artefacts, which Gillis claims to have acquired from Hythloday's own hands and added to the book. These include images of the Utopian alphabet with an example of their language and a poem by the Utopian poet laureate, which identifies Utopia with Plato's republic and gives it the name *eutopia*, for best or most happy place.

Finally, there is the map of Utopia, which appears in both the 1516 and 1518 editions, though much changed between them. The 1516 map is comparatively simple, showing a crescent island, dotted with towers signifying towns, the grandest in the middle. A ship sits at the base, positioned just below the two points of the crescent, with a single individual standing upon it. Other landscapes can be spotted in the distance.

The 1518 map, produced by the noted German artist Ambrosius Holbein, makes the other look cartoon-like in comparison. The rough shape of the island remains, with its towers and central city. Holbein, however, has added more texture to the landscape, such

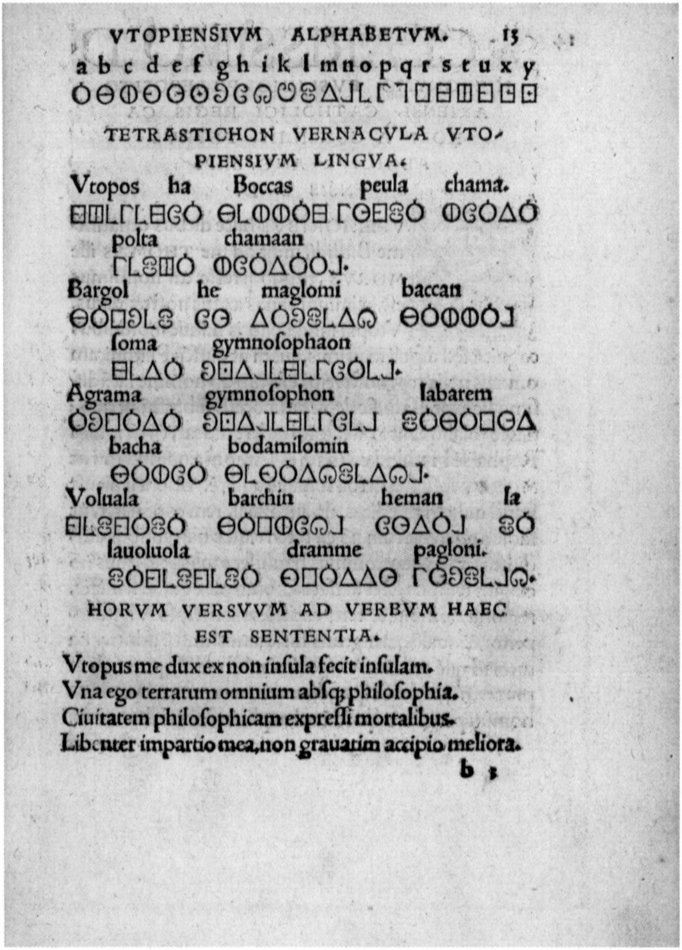

VTOPIENSIVM ALPHABETVM. 13

a b c d e f g h i k l m n o p q r s t u x y

TETRASTICHON VERNACVLA VTO-
PIENSIVM LINGVA.

Vtopos ha Boccas peula chama.
polta chamaan
Bargol he maglomi baccan
ſoma gymnoſophaon
Agrama gymnoſophon labarem
bacha bodamilomin
Voluala barchin heman la
lauoluola dramme pagloni.

HORVM VERSVVM AD VERBVM HAEC
EST SENTENTIA.

Vtopus me dux ex non inſula fecit inſulam.
Vna ego terrarum omnium abſq; philoſophia.
Ciuitatem philoſophicam expreſſi mortalibus.
Libenter impartio mea, non grauatim accipio meliora.

b 3

as rocky crags and forested areas. The labels identifying the central city and river are now suspended from an ornate hanging, which enters the picture from the two topmost corners. The ship is in a mirrored position from the 1516 map, and now flies a flag, which reads 'N.O.R.' reversed. The most obvious changes, however, are the appearance of Hythloday – identified by a label – and two

The Utopian language and alphabet from Thomas More's *Utopia* (1518 edn).

Map of Utopia from Thomas More's *Utopia* (1516 edn).

Map of Utopia by Ambrosius Holbein from Thomas More's *Utopia* (1518 edn).

other figures who must be Morus and Gillis, all of whom stand at the forefront of the image. Hythloday stands in the left-most corner, pointing to the island. Morus stands before him, pointing to Hythloday. Gillis is somewhat removed from this discussion (as he is in Book One's dialogue), to the right-hand corner of the scene.

There are, then, two central images to be parsed in this revised map, produced by an artist closely entwined with the Erasmian humanist circle in Europe. The first is the island itself, with its accompanying ship. As has been pointed out, the placement of the hanging labels, towns and ship, along with the spherical shape of the island, have made it resemble a skull.[51] It is thus a memento mori, a remembrance of death, a common feature of Renaissance art, architecture and iconography. This appearance of Utopia as a skull might seem morbid and out of place for a tale about a fantastical island of equality and happiness, until one remembers the recurrent theme of death running through More's early works, and the reminders of fundamental equality that it brings. As More frequently asserts, death reminds us that we are equal and that nothing truly belongs to us. In death, the stage-play is revealed to be just that, and all those fictions associated with life rot away. The appearance of Utopia as a skull, therefore, reinforces its messages about equality and common property, while still playing with that notion of reality and fiction.

The images of Hythloday, Morus and Gillis are, perhaps, less impactful, though Holbein (almost certainly under Erasmus's, and perhaps More's, direction) thought fit to include them. Like the map, there is a surface meaning; Hythloday points to the island, Morus points to him. More has provided Hythloday's account of Utopia to the masses. However, a closer examination yields a deeper meaning. The pairing of Hythloday and Morus's poses are strongly reminiscent of presentations of Christ and the Doubting Thomas, a tale told in the Gospel of John. St Thomas the Apostle (who shares his name with More) does not believe the other disciples when they tell him that Christ has risen from the dead. Thomas insists that he will not believe until he sees Jesus himself, and touches his wounds with his own hands: 'Jesus saith unto him, Thomas, because thou hast seen me, thou hast believed: blessed are they that have not seen, and yet have believed' (John 20:28–9). In Renaissance depictions of the event, Christ is usually shown with one arm upraised, the other gesturing to the wound on his side in invitation for Thomas to touch it. Thomas, in turn, extends one hand, often a pointed finger, to touch the wound. Hythloday and Morus are found in precisely such a pose. Morus is cast as the doubter, who does not believe that the Christian equality of Utopia is possible on earth. Hythloday asks the reader to believe the truth of Utopia, despite never having seen it and it being contrary to anything one might 'expect' to see possible.

Bringing the two parts of this image together, then, invites the reader to accept the fundamental and yet unseeable reality of Utopia-as-death, a place or state by which all the artificialities of the world pass away. Lived reality is a fiction, *Utopia* tells us; what is real cannot be seen, but must be believed.

Ludovico Mazzolino, *The Incredulity of St Thomas*, *c.* 1522, oil on panel.

FOUR

Writing on Heresy

Thomas More's polemical works against heresy appeared at important stages of his public career as he worked to defend the established Church from the dangers of what he saw as malicious attacks from fanatically deluded opponents: their superficial righteousness provided easy answers for the unwary of weak faith and so threatened to divide the unity of Christendom. More's writings on heresy have a number of interconnected themes, but the central driving issue is the need to preserve the unity of the Church for all Christians and not to allow criticisms of its undoubted individual faults to build up into rebellion and overwhelm the longstanding good of tradition. In many ways More's voluminous writings on heresy are prescient and he accurately saw the danger of the Reformation and how it would bitterly divide Christians. Even so, More's works on the subject, as many commentators have pointed out, are unlikely to prove popular with modern readers.[1] However, there is much to be said for their nature and style, that their repetitiveness, return to the same issues and use of different registers and modes of expression to make almost identical points is a cunning strategy to bring home the seriousness of the threat to true religion, and leave readers in no doubt that concerted action must be taken to counteract the Satanic forces assembled to overwhelm the godly. Furthermore, the dialogue form works to instruct readers and help them defend the Church against its heretical enemies, as well as provide examples of how to argue with those working to overthrow the traditions of the faithful.

More's polemical writing, not surprisingly, takes place during his public career, which lasted from 1516 until his imprisonment in 1534. The discussion of the duties and pains of public office in the first book of *Utopia* serve as a prelude to the reality of More's public career, which involved difficult compromises in his professional life, personal life and writing career, as he worked hard to ensure that Church and government were united within themselves and together against a dangerous common foe, and that the insidious appeal of heretical belief could not tempt a critical mass to inaugurate drastic and irreversible change. That More eventually failed is not a sign of his ineptitude, lack of application or inability to argue effectively; rather, his writings, alongside his actions, might best be viewed as an indication of how well he understood the threat to the Church, the institution which he revered most and which had shaped his life.

More's first major religious polemical work was the *Responsio ad Lutherum* (Response to Luther, 1523), a direct response in Latin to Luther's *Martinus Lutherus contra Henricum Regem Anglia* (Martin Luther against Henry King of England, 1522), which was in turn a reply to Henry VIII's *Assertio Septem Sacramentorum* (Defence of the Seven Sacraments), an assault on Luther's anti-papal writings. For his work Henry received the title of *Fidei Defensor* (Defender of the Faith) from Pope Leo X. More, like Bishop John Fisher, realized that it was his duty to defend the monarch and his Church and produce a show of unity (although it is probably also true, as the story that opens the second edition acknowledges, that he was asked).

More followed his attack on Luther in 1526 with his 'Letter to Johannes Bugenhagen', one of Luther's chief followers, a shorter work that circulated widely in Europe, and which serves as a digest of his views on heresy, the sacraments, faith, free will and

other vital aspects of the faith. He responded to other Protestant works, such as *A Supplication for the Beggars* (1529), in which Simon Fish attacked the heavy taxation imposed by the papacy through indulgences to pay for chantries where prayers could be given for the souls of the dead in Purgatory. More replied with *A Supplication of Souls* that same year, defending the work undertaken by the

Unknown artist, *William Tyndale*, 1681–1741, etching and engraving.

Church to secure salvation for those on their journey to paradise. The 'Letter Against Frith' (1532) is an argument for transubstantiation against John Frith, who had expounded the view of the Swiss reformer Ulrich Zwingli. Zwingli had argued that the sacraments were symbols of Christ's blood and body and that no miraculous transformation took place outside the minds of the congregation. More repeated his defence of orthodox Church teaching on the sacraments – and his attack on the Zwinglian perception of the sacraments – in *The Answer to a Poisoned Book* (1534), a long response to a much shorter anonymous work, *The Supper of the Lord* (1533), now thought to have been written by the reformer George Joye.

That polemical book was the culmination of More's extensive labours to defend the importance of believing in Christ's real presence in the eucharist from the early 1520s onwards. The late 1520s and early 1530s also saw the publication of his major, most substantial attempts to combat heresy. In 1529 *A Dialogue Concerning Heresies* was printed, the work considered by many to be his most successful – and certainly most enjoyable – work on heresy, which has the older More countering the reasonable (but erroneous) arguments of a young student attracted to the arguments of the reformers.[2] More was forcefully critical of the Bible translator William Tyndale, and this disapprobation paved the way for his major assault on Tyndale's thinking and theology, *The Confutation of Tyndale's Answer* (1532–3), which responded to Tyndale's *An Answer to Sir Thomas More's Dialogue* (1530).

Both the *Dialogue* and the *Confutation* were written, like Tyndale's, in English, intermingling learned and colloquial language, arguments and examples to show how widespread he thought the Church's reach should be and how all-pervasive the problem of heresy was, as well as to reach as wide a readership as possible.

LUTHER AND THE PROTESTANTS

The first version of the Latin *Responsio* is narrated by the fictional Ferdinand Baravell, a Spanish student – and so from a country allied to England – who is compelled by his conscience to confront Luther. He recounts that when Luther's works were first circulated at his university there was initially curiosity, 'some men captivated by novelty, others unaware of the new ideas', but the truth eventually dawned on readers that each book written by Luther was worse than the last until 'there finally appeared the *Babylon* [*De captivitate Babylonica Ecclesiae*/On the Babylonian Captivity of the Church], truly that tower of Babel which was built up against heaven, from which the impious fellow undertook to destroy the heavenly sacraments of Christ.'[3] Far from exposing the papacy as a new Babylonian empire, which was Luther's intention, he actually creates confusion, recalling the myth of the origin of languages: arrogant men sought to build a tower up to heaven, which God destroyed in his righteous fury, and then punished the people by preventing them from ever collaborating as successfully again.[4] More's point is that Luther's attempt to return to unity will have the opposite effect entirely and result in long-standing, debilitating divisions, not least the destruction of a common Latin culture by the Bible being translated into the vernacular. Questioning the Church's right to its monopoly over the sacraments will not end well.

Luther was well known for his robust, often scatological, assaults on his opponents, and More demonstrates that he is eager to play Luther at his own game and counter him in kind. He represents Luther as a diabolical mouthpiece, located deep within the Devil's fundament, while Luther imagines he is the closest ally of Christ, exposing himself to universal ridicule:

> Who would not laugh at the most wretched scoundrel blasting out such frenzied boasts, as though he reclined

> on the bosom of Christ, whereas he lies confined within the arse-hole of the devil. Thence he farts and trumpets his splendid victories. Thence he brags that he has conquered the pope, bishops, monks, nuns, masses; and that he has proved all these things to be nothing but sheer monstrosities, idols, phantoms, lies, and the very abomination itself standing in the holy place; and that it is the madness of a sacrilegious people to want to act in the sight of God by works and not by faith alone.[5]

The passage provides a list of flaws and sins that is characteristic of More's polemical approach to heresy, as it enables readers to understand the variety of problems caused by false belief, exemplified, specifically, by Luther imagining that he has successfully attacked the constituents of the Catholic Church whereas in fact he has produced simply a variety of wicked acts.

The passage also signals one of More's principal complaints against Protestantism, one repeated throughout his works against heresy, that it is extremely dangerous to rely on scripture alone. The Protestant rallying cry 'Sola Scriptura' is, for More, an arrogant, empty and self-defeating principle. It might sound reasonable and seem to be a proper Christian goal to strip away the layers of bad practice that have obscured, distorted and lost the original tenets of Christ and his Apostles, as practised in the early Church. However, it is nothing of the sort, as Protestants either forget or ignore the need for the Bible to be interpreted. If the Church and its long traditions of Bible exegesis are cast aside, then all that is left is the individual Christian, helpless and vulnerable, who lacks proper guidance and is therefore likely to lapse into heresy without a community to guide them. For More, scripture demonstrates that the Church is to be trusted and has the right to interpret the Bible, not that the Church is redundant because the individual can carry out this work on their own:

> The Church of Christ did not doubt that whatever the Holy Spirit inspired in the church was undoubtedly true, whether it was contained in scripture or not. Indeed, if any apparently contradictory scriptural text was alleged, the faith written in her heart taught that this text was insufficiently understood by those to whom it seemed so contradictory, since it was a matter of absolute certainty that Christ does not fail his Church on article of faith, nor does the truthful Spirit of God contradict Himself.[6]

After all, it is one of the oldest truths that the Devil reads the Bible rather well and adapts it for his own purposes, one of the central lessons that heresy teaches the true servants of the Church. For More, Satan is a better and more honest reader of the Bible than Luther.[7] More refers to the heretic Faustus of Milevis, who impressed Augustine until they actually met, and the Church Father realized the extent of the apparently holy man's Manicheanism (belief that good and evil struggle for mastery of the universe). Luther is far worse than Faustus, who concluded that everyone who had existed before him was a thief and that 'Moses and the prophets were malefactors.' Luther 'abolishes faith and leaves no certainty in any one at all of the leaders of the old law and the gospel', apart from the clearest of Christ's words, and 'rejects all other men as doubtful . . . because they could have lied, because they were men'.[8]

For More, Protestants have an absurdly misguided and excessive notion of sin, which forces them to be hypercritical of other people and intolerant of any lapses. Instead of the sensible and benign doctrine of 'good works', which decrees that everyone commits sins but that they can atone for these through freely choosing to undertake good works and so restore themselves to God's favour, Protestants believe in 'the elect', those chosen by God to be his true followers and who, therefore, cannot commit sin: if they do sin, it is a clear sign that they are not really one of the elect. In his protracted argument with Tyndale, More suggests there is a vital distinction between Tyndale's use of St Paul's words (in Hebrews 6:4–8) to claim that those who know the true grace of God can never really fall back into sin, and his own belief that those who might sin after baptism are not lost to the faith but 'may after God's help repent again that ever he so did and believe therewithal, that he is bounden to believe and love God and his neighbours as God biddeth him to do'.[9] Just as we should be wary of excessive scepticism in dismissing the testimony of the past, and instead be guided by reason and the wisdom of the Church when trying to understand the writings of God, so we should also realize that humans are weak but inclined to good and not make impossible demands of them or cast them aside when they fail to live up to high standards.

More insists that people need the Church to guide them correctly on their spiritual paths, and the further Protestants move away from the protection and teaching of the Church, the more they will descend into heretical beliefs and practices. There is still time to stop the madness, which is the central hope of the *Dialogue Concerning Heresies*. In that work More argues that Christ wanted his Church to be visible, not hidden, and that it should provide light for the whole world. Alluding to Matthew 5:14 ('You are the light of the world. A town built on a hill cannot be hidden') and probably also to Augustine's *De Civitate Dei* (The City of God), one of More's favourite touchstones, More informs his young charge:

> The city can not be hid that is set on an hill. And he would have his faith divulged & not to revoke his word for bound his preachers to stand thereby & not to revoke his word for no pain. For he said it he did not light the candle to put it & hide it under a bushel/ for so would no man do,

> but he had kindled a fire which he would not should lie & smoulder as coals doth in quenche [that is, when they are doused] but he would it should burn & give light. And therefore folly were it to say if Christ which would have his church spread through the world, & every where gathered in company, would have it turned to a secret unknown single sort, severed a sunder & scattered about in corners/ unknown to all the world.[10]

Expanding Luke 11:33 ('No one lights a lamp and puts it in a place where it will be hidden, or under a bowl. Instead they put it on its stand, so that those who come in may see the light'), More draws out the conclusions of the biblical verse to demonstrate the ludicrousness of God providing man with revelation and then hiding his Church and making the message secret, esoteric and available only to the chosen few. In doing so he reiterates his often-made argument that faith and the chance of salvation are for everyone, through the traditions of the true Catholic Church, and not just for the few, the elect who have somehow met God's standards, as Protestants preach. While Tyndale argued that translating the Bible into English would be a democratic move, fulfilling God's designs for mankind, for More the truly egalitarian position was to support the existing, visible Church, which already contained God's word, interpreted by priests who had been called to dedicate their lives to looking after their congregations. As Augustine had argued, the Church on earth would never be perfect, but it foreshadowed the true Church in heaven and so should be acknowledged as God's authority on earth, the proper way of spreading his message and the bridge between men and women and the afterlife.[11]

THE TRUE CHURCH

More argues that people mistake zealotry for true faith and that the fierce arguments of the heretics sow division and conflict rather than leading people to the truth and light, their passion based on pride rather than humility:

> And thus once proudly persuaded a wrong way, they take the bridle in the teeth and run forth like a head strong horse, that all the world can not pluck them back. But with sowing sedition, setting forth of errors and heresies, and spicing their preaching with rebuking of priesthood and prelacy, for the people's pleasure, they turn many a man to ruin & them self also. And then the devil disguiseth them in their blind affections.[12]

Again, the description is packed with carefully chosen details to convey More's cluster of connections, repeating his message that the true Church leads mankind to faith and salvation, while heresy draws men to damnation. The striking image of the wild horse which has not yet been broken in properly, but which is allowed to lead, is one among many metaphors scattered throughout the *Dialogue*, written in English to reach as wide a readership as possible, its prose frequently signalling the ordinary lives of More's fellow countrymen and women. Not everyone would have been able to ride a horse, but most would, and everyone would have understood the force of this image, a powerful beast charging loose and spreading panic. Connected to the horse metaphor is the picture of the heretical sermon as piquant food, the heretical preacher acting like an ingenious chef rather than a holy figure whose aim is to instruct and enlighten his audience. For More, attacks on the priesthood are simply spicy details designed to appeal to the base instincts of the congregation, perhaps pointing out legitimate flaws and sins, but with no more substance than gossip and hearsay. Furthermore, the image of the heretical preacher as a chef surely recalls Socrates' famous argument that cooking was a false art, especially given Plato's influence on More's Christian humanist thinking, further indicating the subtle and capacious range of More's references.[13] The art of cookery panders to the senses rather than appealing to reason, as philosophy does.

The image cluster demonstrates that one way, that of the true Church, leads to salvation and heaven; the other, Protestant heresy, leads to division, disaster and damnation. The image of the wild horse running free shows that heresy will only get worse and more dangerous if it is unchecked: the more isolated heretics are, the more they become deracinated from the true doctrines of the Church, cut off from debates with the faithful and, as the section cited concludes, a danger to themselves as well as others. This danger is why the Church is justified in sanctioning the extreme punishment of burning unrepentant heretics. After the – relatively – good-natured debate of the *Dialogue*, More concludes with stern warnings to the young student to alert him to the real dangers he will face if he does not abjure his false beliefs, making it clear that he will support such extreme actions to rid heretics from society:

> We read that in the time of saint Austin [Augustine] the great doctor of the church, the heretics of Africa called the Donatists fell to force and violence robbing, beating, tormenting, and killing, such as they took of the true Christian flock, as the Lutherans have done in Almayne [Germany]. For avoiding whereof that holy man saint Austin, which long had with great patience borne and suffered their malice, only done them no temporal harm, but also had letted [prevented] and resisted other that would have done it, did yet at the last for the peace of

> good peace both suffer and exhort the count Boniface and other to repress them with force and fear them with bodily punishment . . . And since that time hath there upon necessity perceived by great outrages committed against the peace & quiet of the people in sundry places of christendom, by heretics rising of a small beginning to an high and unruly multitude, many sore punishments been devised for them and specially by fire.[14]

The authority for the actions More outlines and defends, once again, looks back to Augustine, a patient figure who tried his best to persuade the Donatists, followers of Donatus Magnus, who believed that only a faultless clergy had the power to deliver the sacraments (a belief to which More was especially hostile), to return to the true faith. Unfortunately, when the Donatists continued to resist Augustine's overtures, violently opposing the Church, he had no other recourse than to appeal to Pope Boniface (in office 418–22), who sanctioned the Church's most extreme method of punishment, burning. The symbolic importance of burning heretics, most famously carried out during the reign of Henry VIII's daughter Mary (r. 1553–8), was to cleanse the soul of the heretic, who, it was hoped, would repent while the fire consumed their body, and to purge the realm of false belief, the fire removing all traces of wickedness from the land.[15] For More, heretics brought such extreme punishment on themselves, having always been given the chance to repent, like John Frith, whose arguments against transubstantiation led More to conclude that, if he did not fully recant his views, he deserved to be publicly burned. Frith hid his message in the dark, like heretics everywhere, their beliefs esoteric in the worst possible sense:

> These heretics creep forth among good simple souls, and under a vain hope of some high secret learning, which

> other men abroad either willingly did keep from them, or else could not teach them, they daily with such abominable books corrupt & destroy in corners very many before those writings come unto light, till at the last the smoke of that secret fire beginneth to reek out at some corner, and sometimes the whole fire so flameth out at once, that it burneth up whole towns, and wasteth whole countries.[16]

The thinking of those like Frith may well be secret and dark, but eventually the fire from their tiny candles will light huge conflagrations that will consume cities and countries, unless, of course, the authorities track them down and burn them first. The heretics are, in a proverb all would have known, playing with fire and likely to get burnt.[17]

For More, the Lutherans who rebelled in the German states were also heretics challenging the authority of the Church. More may have known that Luther condemned the peasant revolts strongly, as in *Wider die Mordischen und Reubischen Rotten der Bawren* (Against the Murderous, Thieving Hordes of Peasants, 1525), but the point was that, without repenting of the heresies that had inspired them in the first place, he was personally responsible for the violence. The lone heretic, like the horse veering out of control, eventually causes widespread mayhem if not stopped, by whatever measures are necessary, because with the rejection of good works comes the breakdown of order. The prose carefully leads the reader through the stringent and thoughtful efforts of the Church to stop the spread of heresy until its hand is forced. The warning to the young student tempted to support some of the apparently reasonable ideas and demands of the heretics is clear and stark: if you continue in your false beliefs, you are like the Donatists in Augustine's time, not learning from their dreadful fate, or like the peasants in Germany, inspired by Luther, who cause only violence and suffering, leaving the authorities with no choice but to respond in kind. If you stop now and return to the Church, then the cycle of violence can be ended.

PURGATORY AND ANARCHY

More's response to Simon Fish's *A Supplication of Beggars* (1529), *The Supplication of Souls*, appeared later that same year. Fish's Protestant polemic blamed the greed and excessive authority of the clergy for England's contemporary ills, particularly the high taxes levied by the clergy, along with the sale of indulgences, to pay for Church building projects under the guise of praying for dead souls trapped in Purgatory. Such demands were causing an increase in extreme poverty and in the number of beggars. More's equally acerbic reply defends the Church's record and its role as the champion of the poor, reiterating the need for a Church to oversee the faithful and reaffirming his belief that the proper route to salvation is by performing good works, such as caring for the poor. More sees Fish's intervention as stemming from Luther's heresies, particularly the belief that scripture provides the answer for everything, when in fact the Bible needs careful interpretation. Faith is never enough on its own; it needs to exist within a context: a familiar message in More's works against heresy.

The first book of the treatise concludes with a barnstorming defence of the clergy and an attack on the consequences of allowing Luther's heresy to triumph, delivered like a hellfire sermon, as he ventriloquizes what Fish (whose identity More did not know yet) really meant to write:

> After that the clergy is thus destroyed and cast out, then shall Luther's gospel come in; then shall Tyndale's testament be taken up; Then shall false heresies be preached; then shall the sacraments be set at nought; then shall fasting & prayer be neglected; then shall holy saints be

> blasphemed; then shall almighty god be displeased; then shall he withdraw his grace and let all run to ruin; then shall all virtue be had in derision; then shall all vice reign and run forth unbridled; then shall youth leave labour and all occupation; then shall folk wax idle and fall to unthriftiness; then shall whores and thieves, beggars and bawds increase; then shall [the] unthrifty flock together and swarm about and each bear him bold of other; then shall all laws be laughed to scorn; then shall the servants set nought by their masters, and unruly people rebel against their rulers; then will rise up rifling and robbery, murder and mischief, & plain insurrection, whereof what would be the end, or when you should see it, only God knoweth.[18]

This is another passage in which More demonstrates his skill as a polemicist. The passage imitates contemporary prophecies, which would invariably place the speaker in serious trouble and might even see them face execution, as it had been treason since the Treason Act of 1351 to 'compass' (imagine) the death of the monarch, making prophecy a dangerous art.[19] Here the ventriloquized speaker imagines, not the death of the monarch, but the death and destruction of the Church, which was certainly heresy, if not treason. England will have riots and violence instead of true faith and political order, and sacrilege will proliferate instead of true religion, endangering the souls for whom More is supplicating. The collapse of religion will lead to the collapse of social order as laws are flouted, and the vicious and immoral will thrive so that good farming practices and the sensible accumulation of wealth will be neglected, and all will fall into rack and ruin. The practices of the Church that mark time for the faithful will cease to operate so that the sacraments will be neglected, as will fasting and prayer, and the saints, who not only make up the tradition of the Church but intercede between the people and God, will be cast aside. The world will truly be turned upside down as servants disobey their masters, and in the absence of officers upholding the law, there will be anarchy.

More forces his readers to imagine a future in which nothing that makes up the world in which they all live exists any longer. It is a nightmarish vision of chaos and destruction, designed to show that the demands made by critics of the Church – that the Bible be translated into the vernacular, that the Church not exploit its congregations, that the clergy justify their status as a privileged elite, and so on – only seem reasonable to those who have not yet thought deeply enough about their implications. In fact, as a learned defender of the Church can point out, they will have effects that are far worse than most can imagine, and certainly worse than anyone could want.

In line with his attack on the limitations of simply believing that faith is all a Christian needs, More provides a series of robust defences of the importance of saints and the miracles that took place to sanctify many of them. In his gargantuan polemic against Tyndale, More seizes on a quotation from his opponent that confirms that many of the prophets were witnesses to miracles when they were not preaching the gospel. More agrees, but uses their apparent accord to attack Tyndale's assumptions:

> It followeth that since holy preachers and miracles were always so necessary in the other, that god always provides them so plenteously, that they never lacked: he hath in likewise all this while provided, that in his own church holy preachers and miracles have also continued and have never lacked. And then followeth further, that sith in all this while there hath never been in any church of heretics (as many as have been of them) neither saint nor miracle, but both twain ever plenteously continued in this only

> church, which is the common known catholic church of christ.[20]

Miracles, according to More, are a testimony of God's grace and serve to validate the existence of this Church on earth. Their continuation after the claims of the heretical Protestants shows that the Catholic Church is indeed the true Church. Miracles have always occurred and have taken place alongside the preaching of the Bible by its prophets to demonstrate that their interpretation of God's word has his blessing, a sign to the faithful that they can believe what they have heard. Protestants, according to More, do not have miracles: More infers that this is because they are cut off from God, not because all they need is scripture, as they claim. For More, the existing Church makes logical sense and reason will lead believers to it, as they will understand that it is in line with God's revelation, a Christian humanist message that he had outlined in *Utopia*. The passage cited above deliberately follows traditional scholastic logic in outlining causes, one proposition leading to another and showing how thinking carefully about belief demonstrates that everything has a consequence. Just as true belief can build on what God has given us, reason and revelation leading the true Christian to understand the logical nature of the mysteries of the faith, so heresy leads to false, dangerous and seditious conclusions that do not follow causes, but which feed on delusions to destroy both religion and society.

More's sustained attack on Tyndale's theology and Bible translation demonstrates how great he perceived Tyndale's threat to the established Church to be, which is a further sign of More's prescience and ability to understand his opponents. After all, as many commentators have pointed out, Tyndale's translation lies behind every subsequent English translation of the Bible, most significantly the 1611 King James version.[21] More's *Confutation*, angry and dismissive as it is, is testament to the powerful danger that he recognized in Tyndale's words as well as his personality.

THE THREAT OF TRANSLATION

More might be seen to surrender some ground to Tyndale, or, at least, to be embarrassed about aspects of the Church's history. More had a bitter and protracted argument with Tyndale about the translation of the Greek word *ekklesía* and whether it could be rendered in English as 'church' or 'congregation', notably in biblical verses such as Matthew 16:18, which Tyndale translated as 'Upon this rock I will build my congregation,' which is 'the first attempt in the English language to supplant *church* in its sense of a body of Christians'.[22] More, not surprisingly, concentrated on Tyndale's change as a key feature of their dispute, recognizing the importance of the change in meaning from the institution of the Church to any gathering of Christians (following Matthew 18:20, 'For where there are two or three gathered together in my name, there am I in the midst of them'). More responds angrily to Tyndale's translation, claiming that he has removed the significance of the most important word in the Christian lexicon, the one that defines the nature of the institution that unites Christians, and overthrown one and a half millennia of Christian practice:

> But now that thing the good folk have of good mind bygone, and many hundred years continued, Tyndale as one of another sort would have utterly changed, and rather then lay men should have any such reverent mind to priests as to call them the church, he would take it from them both, and putting away from both that holy name of church, would call them both by the name of congregation, a word without any signification of christendom any more than of Jews or Turks.[23]

Tyndale is a revolutionary like Luther, his heresy catapulting the Church into a brave and frightening new world from which all the old traditions and certainties have been suddenly removed, leaving people lost and confused. More cleverly suggests that it is both priests and laymen who cannot comprehend the changes that Tyndale wishes to make, indicating that the Protestant desire to break down distinctions between the two in the name of 'the priesthood of all believers' fails spectacularly and has the opposite effect as all are cut off from the Church rather than being united within it. The institution is effectively reduced to a relatively meaningless descriptive term of no more value than any of the institutions and offices that bind Jews and Turks (Muslims) together as believers in false religions that Christians are duty bound to oppose and convert.

However, it is worth noting that later in the *Confutation* More sidesteps the question of whether the pope's leadership is inherently bound up with his conception of the Church: 'For the avoiding of all intrycacyon [complication, entanglement] whereof/ I purposely forbeare to put in the pope as part of the definition of the church, as a thing that needed not, sith if he be the necessary head, he is included in the name of the whole body.'[24] Given More's care with definitions and logical consequences, the conditional 'if' seems very significant indeed. The office of the pope may be bound up within the Church if that is how the Church is defined, leaving open the possibility that the Church could be defined in other ways that do not necessarily involve the papacy. And More's working definition of the Church concentrates on the body and cluster of the Christians within it, not its formal hierarchy, making his Church sound very like Tyndale's congregation, a word he uses: 'I wist [know] very well that the church being proved this common known catholic congregation of all christian nations, abiding together in one faith, neither fallen of nor cut off.'[25] In an obvious way More's definition is a response to Tyndale, taking the word 'congregation' and placing it back in its proper place within the Church. But in other ways it shows that Christian intellectuals like More and Tyndale sometimes had more in common than they or anyone else might have assumed.

For More, the Church agrees on common doctrine and provides a unified message for all Christians in contrast to the divisive doctrines of Luther and Tyndale, marking them and their fellow travellers out as heretics:

> Yet this one mark alone of the old holy doctors of the catholic church, condemning the heresies of Tyndale and Luther and all their other sects, clearly would give a light, by which the true doctrine might be known from the false. And therefore this mark alone as openly as marked Luther, & Tyndale . . . and all the rabble of their fellows, for open & plain heretics, as if the devil had his own hands marked each of them an .H. in the forehead, with a fair hot iron fetched out of the fire of hell.[26]

Just as the light of the true doctrine of the Church shines brightly and clearly in contrast to the dark, secret candle of heresy, so the Church is able to point out those most dangerous to its unity and bring them into full view as if they had been marked by the Devil himself, branded like common criminals (which, for More, they have been). More deliberately exaggerates the unity of the Church because there had been important arguments between Church Fathers, such as the well-known series of disputes between Augustine and Jerome about the canon and interpretation of the Bible. But his point stands: whatever the disagreements, they are simply differences and remain, by definition, within the confines of the institution of the Church itself, quite distinct from the battles with heresy that Augustine, to name only the most obvious example, was engaged in as he sought to combat the Donatists and the Manicheans.

In More's view the true Church will always survive no matter what happens because it is God's will that it does. In the *Dialogue Concerning Heresies*, More argues that, in significant matters, the Church cannot misread the Bible and distort the Christian message, as he admonishes his young interlocutor for doubting its authority:

> The church can not misunderstand the scripture to the hinderance of the right faith, in things of necessity, and that ye also knowledge this matter to be such, that it must either be the right belief and acceptable service to god, or else a wrong and erroneous opinion and plain idolatry, it followeth of necessity, that the church doth not misunderstand those texts, that ye or any other can allege, and bring forth for that purpose. But that all these texts be so to be taken and understood as they nothing make against the church, but all against your own opinion in this matter.[27]

More uses the language of scholastic logic to show that one consequence follows from another and that the Church, therefore, cannot err. The reasoning he deploys is essentially circular: the Church interprets scripture correctly, therefore whatever the Church decrees is true. Again, More contrasts the weight of the Church's traditions and practices with the isolated and fragile response of the lone heretic, a strategy that might seem both comforting and bullying at the same time. If the student comes back into the fold, then they can be looked after, their errors corrected and a good Christian life followed by salvation assured. More consistently defines the Church as a community of like-minded thinkers who iron out any important differences and preserve a united front on doctrine, not a hierarchical structure that issues commands. Anyone who has lapsed can return to the Church as long as they accept that it has a monopoly on truth: 'if ye will in faith or living or avoiding of all damnable error (that ye might fall in by misunderstanding of scripture) take a sure and infallible way/ *ye must in all these things here/ believe & obey the church.*'[28]

More is not against the translation of the Bible into English as such, acknowledging that many people want to read it and should be able to do so. The problem is that the existing translations – those of Tyndale and Wycliffe – are heretical and will lead readers to damnation rather than salvation. They make no distinction between priests and laity, Tyndale following Luther in claiming that 'a priest is nothing else, but a man chosen among the people to preach,' not the holder of a sacred office.[29] It follows, therefore, that 'every man woman and child may do as well as any priest,' which, for More, destroys the foundations of the Church and places it in the hands of any heretic who wishes to assert power over the congregation.[30] People need to trust the words of the Church Fathers and not be misled by those of the newly fashionable heretics. In Tyndale's translation the priesthood has been devalued and reduced to nothing, which is why his version cannot be tolerated: 'in all his translation where so ever he speaketh of them, the name of priest which is to us in our own tongue hath always signified an anointed person and with holy orders consecrated unto god, he hath changed into the name of senior [elder] no word of our language.'[31] Instead of a caste of truly faithful servants dedicated to preserving the Church as God's authority on earth, Tyndale portrays them as self-appointed and self-important figures with no loyalty to anyone. More dwells on the issue of translation, central to Reformation disputes and conflicts.[32] While the term 'priest' has a proper place within the English language and is recognized by native speakers, the heretics have introduced a meaningless foreign term, 'elder', that no one but they can understand. Not only are they seeking to fracture the unity of the Church, but they are separating Church and people from their native traditions and making what should be central to everyone's existence, the Church, strange and alien. This is another reason why More's major works on heresy are written in English.

TRUE FAITH

If the Church, priests and the very language of the nation are to be cast aside, then so will all the traditions, rituals and practices that bind English communities together, a serious and deep-seated fear as the work of Eamon Duffy has demonstrated.[33] In the *Responsio ad Lutherum*, More rails against Luther's desire to expunge the images of saints and martyrs from churches, an error that will remove a significant layer of protection and certainty from the individual seeking to repent for their sins:

> Because Luther has so little care for the martyrs that he argues that their images and veneration should be wholly abolished, I desire at least to know this of him – if he admits nothing at all besides evident scriptures – what sufficiently clear answer he would give if, when he promises such easy remission of all sins by faith alone, and that by means of any sort of sudden penitence lasting but a moment, someone were to bring up that text about the sin against the Holy Spirit which Christ clearly says is not to be forgiven either in this world or in the next?[34]

In contrast to the hard labour of atonement through good works, Luther provides Christians with the promise of instant redemption after repentance, leading to licentiousness rather than liberty. But the promise rests on shaky foundations, something that is simultaneously easy and terrifying because there can be no certainty that God has forgiven the sinner without the guarantee of the Church's promises. More is appealing to the brightly coloured interiors of late medieval churches with their images of saints to reassure Christians that God had created a large community of past and present believers to protect and nurture Christians. In contrast to the long and stable traditions of the Church, the heretics rely on sudden moments of transformation, which no one can ever be sure are not delusional or diabolical.

Familiar doctrines such as the belief in purgatory are also defended. In *The Supplication of Souls*, More compares the pains of purgatory to seasickness, unpleasant but hardly deadly. Some, who have not sinned much, will not be affected much but will be 'as lusty and as jocund as if they were on land'; others will find that 'one vomit or twain so clean rid of their grief, that they never feel displeasure of it after'; but most will, More acknowledges, not be quite so lucky, and they will 'walter & tolter' and 'wring their hands, and gnash the teeth, and their eyen water, their head ache, their body frete [be consumed with worry], their stomach wamble, and all their body shiver for pain'.[35] The demotic description is comforting, demonstrating to readers that it is better to enter purgatory in a state of relative grace so that suffering is reduced to a minimum, but that it will not be a terrifying ordeal for most and will resemble a necessary risk accepted by any traveller.

The most important rite in the everyday Christian calendar was the eucharist. More provides a number of defences of the Church's doctrine of transubstantiation throughout his writings, appealing to the traditional beliefs and community of Christians against the assaults of heresy. This culminated in his treatise *The Answer to a Poisoned Book*, the title of which demonstrates how much More thought was at stake in the dispute. Infuriated by the argument that the sacraments should be seen no more than symbolic, More provided a lengthy, polemical defence of the real presence of Christ in the eucharist, arguing that any attack on this central facet of the Church's identity threatened its existence by denigrating the sacred power of the priesthood and their right to administer the sacraments, leaving the congregation without proper leadership to cohere as a group of the faithful and therefore vulnerable to heresy. Again, the work was written in English to reach a wide audience, making use of familiar examples to demonstrate that the Church, represented by More, was not obsessively hierarchical and cut off from the common people, and that it was the Protestants, who claimed the priesthood of all believers, who were, in fact, the elitists. More is clear that the Bible does not need to be read allegorically when Jesus referred to the faithful eating his body and drinking his blood: 'For every man may here well see . . . that Christ in those words [John 6:53–7] beside all parables and allegories, spake and meant of the very eating of his very flesh in deed.'[36] The Church is united in reading the text in the same way, in contrast to the lone heretical voice of the author of *The Supper of the Lord*: 'there are against master masker [the anonymous author] not only the catholic church of our time, but also all the old holy doctors and saints, which with *one voice* expound these words of Christ to be spoken and meant of that eating of Christ's flesh.'[37] It is only heretics like the anonymous author and John Frith who seek to undermine the truth of traditional belief.

More's works against heresy are long and wordy, returning time and again to the same themes. For many readers this makes them tedious, and little to More's credit. Certainly, More felt the need to put his considerable literary and polemical talents to the service of the Church and State after he agreed to take public office, so it is clear that these works really mattered to him. A case for the defence would argue that they are long and repetitive because they are trying to make readers understand what is at stake in arguments that could seem relatively trivial if they are not properly explained. If one way of putting an argument fails to persuade a particular reader, there will be other chances to learn the message later in the text, and the *Confutation* might best be read as a reference work, a storehouse of arguments and examples that could be used to combat heresy. The same applies to a reader missing a point the first time around. For More, the arguments are not about the minutiae of doctrine but about the Church's right and need to intercede between God and mankind and for readers to understand that anything that threatened that relationship was dangerous heresy. More's works deliberately mix theological arguments with examples drawn from the everyday life of the people that the clergy were committed to serve, showing that the Church was by their side and at their level, even as the priesthood had to be distinguished as a separate class devoted to the service of God. As in most great literary disputes, More and his opponents often sound similar and adopt similar tactics in their arguments and their language. That More expended so much energy in a losing cause has only contributed to his posthumous reputation.

CRAN
MER

FIVE

Oath of Supremacy, Trial and Late Spiritual Writings

There is some confusion, when speaking about the fall and final years of Thomas More, about precisely to what he died in opposition. What oath did he refuse – succession or supremacy – and why? The perplexity is understandable. There was confusion at the time as to the wording of the oaths, waters that have only become further muddied by the passage of time and More's own dedication to silence in the year between his arrest and his execution.[1] The fact remains that the succession and the supremacy were intertwined in the minds of those seeking to accomplish both, as well as in their actual execution. Without recognizing Henry VIII as Supreme Head of the English Church, his marriage to Anne Boleyn and their child, Elizabeth, were rendered illegitimate. Recognizing the altered succession required recognizing that Henry VIII had the power to dissolve a marriage sanctioned by the pope. More's own approach doesn't help, as he got around this entanglement by asserting the authority of Parliament over the matter of the succession. In other words, he was content to recognize the succession but not the supremacy, yet it was his refusal to swear the oath of succession for which he was arrested. It was denying the supremacy for which he was executed.

A careful reading of More's statements – largely written but some spoken – on the matter in the last fifteen months of his life helps to disentangle almost five centuries of confusion, though not

'The Pope suppressed by Henry VIII', hand-coloured woodcut from John Foxe, *Actes and Monuments* (1570).

entirely. The messiness of this question reflects the messiness of the time, the slapdash way in which Henry VIII's supremacy was enacted and enforced over a few short years, and how opposition like More's was done away with as swiftly as possible, with little regard for precise legalities. In his defence, More combined a commitment to these legalities with the adoption of silence, a strategy he came to during his imprisonment, drawn from both his knowledge of the law and his reading of scripture.[2]

Henry VIII first asserted his supremacy of the English Church in early 1531, adding a clause to a subsidy agreement with Convocation. Convocation had been tasked with deciding between accepting that all its members – the entire English clergy – were guilty of *praemunire* (maintaining papal jurisdiction) or paying the king a £100,000 penalty, a sum equivalent to the entire annual income of the crown.[3] Resisting the king's threats, Convocation agreed to the financial penalty, though it added a prologue to the agreement, framing the payment as a gracious token of their esteem to the king for his defence of the 'Universal Church' against any who would wish to 'blemish and hurt the estimation of the said prelates and clergy'.[4] It was to this prologue that Henry VIII insisted be added a recognition of his role as 'sole protector and supreme head of the Anglican Church and clergy'. After much debate, Convocation agreed, though it added the clause 'as far as the law of Christ allows'.[5] This amended agreement passed, though only because the members of Convocation remained silent, allowing its leader, William Warham, to assume that *qui tacet consentire videtur* ('he who is silent is taken to consent'), a legal precedent to which More would later appeal.

In early 1531 none of this had anything directly to do with Thomas More, whose only role was to oversee the agreement's ratification in the House of Lords in his position as Lord Chancellor. There was no question, however, that he opposed it. Eustace Chapuys, Charles V's ambassador to England, reported that More was 'so displeased' with these developments that 'he desires to be out of his office.'[6] Roper gives a similar account, that it was around this time that More approached the Duke of Norfolk, asking him 'to be a means to the King that he might, with His Grace's favour, be discharged' of the office of Lord Chancellor.[7]

More later wrote at length, in his *Apology*, about the need to keep the spiritual and temporal spheres apart.[8] They worked together like 'the soul and the body', separate but in congress. If they did not, 'the dregs of both sorts conspiring together and increasing, may little and little grow too strong for both,' severing the connection and thus – having divided – conquering 'the good people of both'.[9] More saw this dissolution of the divide between temporal and spiritual in the Submission of the Clergy, in May 1532, when Convocation fully submitted to the control of the king. He resigned the following day. More claimed the reason was his health, which may indeed have been failing.[10] But Chapuys, among others, recognized it was a problem not of the body, but of the soul.[11]

More said little on the supremacy or the succession in the years following his resignation. Notably, though, he reinforced his position on the pope, which was equivocal, at best. Although the pope had been 'recognized and knowledged' by all nations as the 'successor of Saint Peter' and thus the head of the Church, More deftly avoided defending this position at length.[12] Instead, his emphasis was on the General Council, as the representative and governing body of the Church. The General Council was directly analogous to other representative bodies, such as Parliament, albeit with a greater jurisdiction and authority.[13] The Council had the 'like strength and power' of the entire Church, 'as if they had been assembled', in the same way that Parliament had the authority of the entire realm.[14]

He did also comment on the question of obedience, in a rare moment of agreement with Tyndale and his followers. 'They say', and More agreed, 'that the laws & precepts of their sovereigns do nothing bind the subjected in their consciences,' if those things 'were before commanded or forbidden in Scripture'.[15] Jesus commanded obedience to secular authorities but did not mean 'that they should obey any commandment that by God were forbidden, nor set God's law aside for men's traditions'.[16] More agreed with Tyndale that a conscientious subject might legitimately refuse a ruler's command, if it contradicted God's Word. The two men simply differed on the interpretation of that Word and, more importantly, on who was doing the interpreting. For Tyndale, More asserted, it was left to individuals. More maintained that it rested with the Church, which he defined as the entire community of believers, across time and space, expressed through mechanisms such as the General Council.

Both the establishment of the supremacy and changes to the succession picked up speed in 1533. On Passion Sunday of that year, Henry VIII installed Thomas Cranmer as Archbishop of Canterbury. Presiding over a submissive Convocation, within two days they ruled that Catherine of Aragon had consummated her relationship with Prince Arthur, making her marriage to Henry VIII illegitimate. By Easter, churches across the realm were praying for King Henry and Queen Anne, whom the king had secretly married earlier in the year. With Cranmer ruling Convocation, in Cromwell's capable hands Parliament was also cutting through years of delays. The Act of Restraint in Appeals was before the House of Commons in March. In essence, the bill set out that it was the king, not the pope, who was the final authority in all Church matters in England, and any appeal to papal authority would be, henceforth, illegal. Queen Anne was crowned in May and, whether or not More actually gave his prophetic speech about being 'deflowered' and then 'devoured', there is no record of his attendance. Anne gave birth to a daughter in September, Elizabeth, and the project of ensuring she was

Gerlach Flicke, *Thomas Cranmer*, 1545, oil on panel.

Henry VIII's legal heir – thus supplanting his daughter by Catherine of Aragon, Mary – began.

The Act of Succession was introduced to the House of Lords on the Friday before Passion Sunday, 1534. It outlined the new succession, but the preamble also asserted Henry VIII's supremacy and reduced the pope to the position of Bishop of Rome. The oath was built into the act, with the punishment of misprision of treason for those who 'obstinately refuse' to swear. More, it appears, recognized this instantly as a legal sword pointed at him, placing his property into a trust two days after the act passed the Lords. After it passed the Commons, More signed over 1 hectare (2½ ac) of his Chelsea property to his eldest daughter and her husband.

Later, in the Tower, More recorded that it occurred to him at this time that he 'might put my body in peril of death by refusing of this oath', a prospect which terrified him, as he warred between the 'saving of my body' and 'the loss of my soul'.[17] He emerged from this internal turmoil resolute that 'it is a case in which a man may lose his head and yet have none harm, but instead of harm inestimable good at the hand of God.'[18] He would not, however, say why he considered the oath to be contrary to his conscience, and worth risking his life.

More was summoned in April 1534 to take the oath at Lambeth Palace, before a commission which included the new Lord Chancellor, Thomas Audley, the dukes of Suffolk and Norfolk and the Archbishop of Canterbury, Cranmer. What remains unclear, however, is the content of the oath to which he was asked to swear. There were several oaths circulating in early 1534, which all differed to a greater or lesser degree. There was every chance, as well, that More was asked to swear an additional clause, which was being issued to the clergy also called to Lambeth that day, that 'the Bishop of Rome had no greater authority in England than any other foreign bishop.'[19] There was nothing stopping the commissioners from adding this line to More's oath.

Most likely, he was asked to swear to the wording that had been accepted by Parliament at the end of March. It included three clauses to which More might have objected. The first was an acknowledgement of Henry's heirs as set out in the Act of Succession: Elizabeth (and any other of Anne's children) before Mary. The second was that the oath-taker's 'Faith, Truth and Obedience' were to be borne alone to the king and these heirs and not to 'any other within this Realm, nor foreign Authority, Prince or Potentate', easily interpreted as the pope. Finally, the oath-taker was to 'observe, keep, maintain and defend' the Act of Succession 'and all the Contents and Effects thereof', which included the king's supremacy. This clause also set out that they were to defend 'all other Acts and Statutes made since the Beginning of this present Parliament', which included a host of anticlerical measures passed since it was first convened in 1529. More reported that he read over the text of the oath carefully and asked to read the text of the Act of Succession before he answered.

More's refusal was carefully couched, as he described in a letter to Margaret, written soon after he was installed in the Tower. He 'would not deny to swear to the Succession' but would not swear 'unto the oath that there was offered me, without jeoparding of my soul to perpetual damnation'.[20] Was, then, the line specifically repudiating the authority of the 'Bishop of Rome' added to More's oath? Or did he mean that he would swear to the succession itself but not the whole text of the oath, with those other objectionable clauses? Later that day, he offered to set out his reasons in writing, if the commissioners could promise he would not be punished for doing so. The commissioners, however, could not guarantee that such a declaration would not fall foul of the terms of the act, and so More answered that 'if I may not declare the causes without peril, then to leave them undeclared is no obstinacy.'[21]

In this first encounter, and in this early Tower letter, More set out his view of his position vis-à-vis the Act of Succession. 'If there were no more but myself upon my side and the whole Parliament upon the other', then he would indeed be 'sore afraid to lean to mine own mind only against so many'.[22] But in regard to the reasons of his refusal, which he still would not name, he had 'upon my part as great a council and greater too', and so he was not required to change his conscience on the matter 'and conform it to the council of one realm against the General Council of Christendom'.[23]

More was imprisoned for his refusal to swear to the oath of the succession, though his objections to it seemed to have more to do with the king's claims to the supremacy. In response, Henry's ministers played with the idea of formally separating these entangled issues. The week after More's first interview, Cranmer wrote to Cromwell, reminding him that 'my Lord of Rochester [John Fisher] and Master More were contented to be sworn to the act of the king's Succession, but not to the preamble of the same,' though he expressed uncertainty as to the cause of their refusal, whether it stemmed from 'the diminution of the authority of the Bishop of Rome' or 'the reprobation of the king's first pretensed matrimony'.[24] Cranmer recommended a

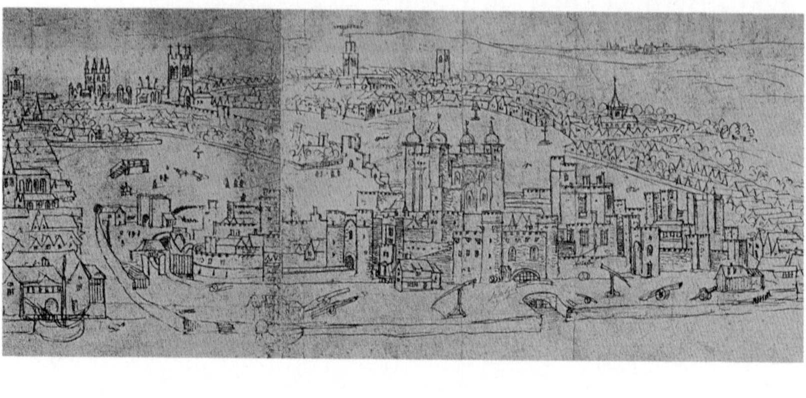

View of the Tower of London, detail from panorama drawing by Anton van den Wyngaerde, *c.* 1543–50.

compromise. They should, he suggested, accept an oath to the 'very Act of Succession', minus the preamble, as long as they would also swear to the clause about 'all powers and potentates'. This would be a major propaganda victory for the crown, Cranmer set out, showing that the king's marriage and the act were 'according to God's laws'.

Henry, however, when Cromwell showed him Cranmer's letter, was not impressed. He worried about the precedent set for others by separating the act from its preamble. The two issues, Henry maintained, could not be set apart in the way that Cranmer proposed, as it 'might be taken not only as a confirmation of the Bishop of Rome his authority, but also a reprobation of the king's second marriage'.[25] As such, More and Fisher must be sworn 'as well to the preamble as to the Act of Succession' or else it might be 'an utter destruction to his whole cause'. The entanglement of the supremacy and the succession was necessary to the establishment of each, and More would remain in the Tower until he acknowledged both.

Early into his imprisonment, More and his daughter began an elaborate epistolary game. According to Roper, this began with Margaret, who wrote her father a letter 'wherein she seemed somewhat to labour to persuade him to take the oath', though it was not what she really believed.[26] It was a ruse to 'get liberty to have free resort unto her father'. More, on receiving it, performatively upbraided her for her 'lamentable letter' and reminded her that he would not give the reasons for not swearing the oath.[27] Both knew that Cromwell was reading every word that passed between them. In any case it worked, and Margaret was allowed to visit her father in the Tower.

It has been suggested that More's best-known Tower work, *The Dialogue of Comfort Against Tribulation*, was a product of time spent in discussion with the scholarly Margaret. He set his dialogue in Hungary, recently invaded by the Turks, and created two central interlocutors, one younger and one older. The elder, Antony, was a learned octogenarian; the younger, Vincent, was Antony's 26-year-old nephew, who pleaded with his uncle to share his wisdom as the Turks threatened. Antony was undoubtedly the voice of authority, through which More articulated his arguments about the nature of life, death and suffering. Vincent may have been inspired by Margaret, or More's own nephew William Rastell, who was of an age with More's invented interlocutor.

The dialogue is a meditation on how to face suffering, especially religious persecution. For the most part, More's foreign fictionalized context ensures that the dialogue does not touch on his own circumstances, though there are flashes of relevance in the text that are difficult to overlook. Antony sets out that position and fortune should not be shunned, as they can be used for the common good, but 'if one perceiveth that in wealth and authority he doth his own soul harm,' and what was required of him leads to decay and ruin, 'then I would in any wise advise him to leave off that thing' – that office – 'and rather give it over quite and draw himself aside, and serve God,' rather than to 'take the worldly worship and commodity for himself, with incommodity of them whom his duty were to profit'.[28] It was precisely the choice that More had made in resigning the Chancellorship.

A lesser-known Tower dialogue is contained in a letter written by More (and likely Margaret) to his stepdaughter Alice Allington. It takes More and Margaret directly as the interlocutors, as they debate Allington's news that the new Lord Chancellor, Thomas Audley, has little sympathy for his predecessor's plight. Calling Margaret 'Mistress Eve' and Alice the 'serpent' for their attempt to 'tempt your father again' to 'swear against his conscience, and so send him to the devil', he chides Margaret for returning to a topic they have discussed more 'often than twice or thrice'.[29] Each time he has told her 'that in this matter if it were possible for me to do the thing that might content the King's Grace, and God therewith not offended, there hath no man taken this oath more gladly than I would do'.[30] Having 'many years studied' the issue, however, he knows full well it does not sit with his conscience, and is ready to suffer the consequences.

He remains oblique about what precisely rubs his conscience the wrong way, but to Margaret's objection that the oath is administered by 'a law made by the Parliament commanded', he returns that the law is binding 'upon some temporal pain', but it does not mean that the laws are well made or in accordance with God's laws.[31] 'I put you the case', More continues, in his manner from his time as a student of the law, if a law is made 'in any particular part of Christendom', over which there is dispute as to its standing vis-à-vis God's law, 'I can see none that lawfully may command and compel any man to change his own opinion and to translate his own conscience from the one side to the other.'[32] More appeals to the doctrine of obedience he had set out in response to – and in rare agreement with – Tyndale. If a law contradicts God's law, a man is not required to hazard his soul in obedience to it, though he must take the temporal, bodily punishment in his stride.

This did not mean, More sets out in his *Sadness of Christ* – a lengthy reflection on the suffering that preceded Christ's capture and death on the cross – that they must be faced without fear. Some, it was true, would suffer and die for Christ's sake without fear and face their deaths smiling. But others would undergo 'fearful anxiety' and be 'deeply distressed' with 'fear and trembling'.[33] There was, More argued, no 'stigma of guilt' to experience 'the fear of death and torments'. On the contrary, 'the brave man bears up under the blows which beset him,' whereas 'the senseless man simply does not feel them when they strike.' To try to escape death was foolish, but to fear it was sensible. To face it despite fear for a godly cause counted one among the saints.

When Parliament reconvened for its sixth session in early November 1534, its most important piece of business was to pass the Act of Supremacy, which codified what had already been established regarding the king's supremacy over the Church. The oath passed was not precisely that which had been sworn by Parliament in its spring session, but one which included more specific reference to repudiating 'foreign authority'. According to Roper, 'the Lord Chancellor and Master Secretary' – Audley and Cromwell – 'did of their own heads add more words unto' the Oath, before it was administered to More, which had caused More to question the legality of his imprisonment.[34] This passing of the oath in November legitimized More's imprisonment by enshrining into law the version of the oath he had refused to take.[35]

This still only made More guilty of misprision of treason. The new Treason Act, however, introduced into the Lords in November 1534, redefined what constituted treason.[36] Whereas it had previously been treason to attempt to bring about the death of the king, queen or heir, this was now expanded to include those who 'wish, will or desire by words of writing' any harm to these royal persons 'or to deprive them of any of their dignity or title' as well as to call the king 'heretic, schismatic, tyrant, infidel or usurper'. As John Rastell, More's brother-in-law but now a client of Cromwell, remembered it, some of the Commons' fear was assuaged by emphasizing that these words must be uttered 'maliciously'.[37]

More had already embraced a strategy of silence in regard to his reasons for refusing the oath, only being willing to utter them if he was promised legal protections. The new Treason Act made such protections impossible and any utterance in objection to the Succession or Supremacy Act treason. What's more, he found a spiritual reinforcement for this policy in his reading of the Psalms. The 'meek man' in tribulation must 'neither speak

Thomas More's prayer book, which he was allowed to keep while imprisoned in the Tower of London, with his annotations.

proudly nor retort wicked words, but instead he should bless the evil-speakers and suffer patiently either for the sake of justice if he has deserved it, or, if he has not deserved it, for the sake of God.'[38] Though friends and neighbours 'did violence which sought my soul' and 'spake vanities, and meditated guiles', the psalmist responds 'as one deaf, did not hear: and as one dumb not opening his mouth'.[39] 'I was dumb and humbled,' More wrote next to another passage, 'and kept silence.'

He stuck to this strategy over the interrogations that began in April 1535. When asked by Cromwell to declare his opinion of the Act of Supremacy, More responded that he had already given his views to the king and to Cromwell and would no longer 'dispute king's titles nor popes'.[40] He would 'never meddle in the world again, to have the world given me', and his whole study would be 'upon the Passion of Christ and mine own passage out of this world', the two works on which he laboured in the Tower. At his next interrogation, More told Margaret that it was clear the commissioners' whole purpose was 'either to drive me to say precisely the one way, or else precisely the other', and he refused to do either.[41] He 'would make none answer' to the question of whether he thought the Act of Supremacy was lawful.

This was not quite true, however, and in the course of the interrogation – even according to his own account – he reiterated that he considered the Act of Supremacy to be counter to the laws of God, expressed by the Universal Church. 'In this case,' he told Cromwell, 'a man is not by a law of one realm so bound in his conscience, where there is a law of the whole corps of Christendom to the contrary.' It was a matter of legal jurisdictions, as well as conscience. The notaries present at the interview recorded this response as an answer to the question of the Act's legality: that 'if he said that the same law were good, then it was dangerous to the soul. And if he said contrary to the said statute, then it was death to the body.'[42] More might not have given his reasons, but he had not avoided declaring that he considered the act unlawful, despite his claims to silence.

About a week later, Cromwell had the final piece of evidence necessary to suggest that More fell foul of the new Treason Act. A fellow lawyer, Richard Rich, was sent with two men to deprive More of his books and papers. They engaged in a game of putting of cases. There are three possible accounts of this discussion, one More's, the second Rich's and the third another version from Rich, possibly altered by Cromwell. According to More, there were two scenarios and questions put to him by Rich. First, that an act of parliament made Rich king. More agreed that he would accept, in such a scenario, that Rich was king for 'Parliament may well, Master Rich, meddle with the state of temporal princes.' Second, that an act of parliament made Rich the pope. To this, More implied that Parliament lacked the jurisdiction to make this statute, and he responded with a case of his own, that 'Parliament would make a law that God should not be God.' Rich agreed that this parliament could not do. More used this agreement to answer Rich's second case: 'No more could the Parliament make the king Supreme Head of the Church,' meaning the Universal Church – the position of pope – and not Supreme Head of the Church of England.

Rich recorded the conversation with More, but his account differs slightly from More's recollection. According to Rich, More immediately went from the initial kingly case to the question of Parliament ruling 'that God were not God', and it was Rich who put the 'middle case' about making the king head of the Church.[43] According to Rich, More responded that 'although the king were accepted' as such 'in England, yet most outer parts do not affirm the same.' This was a significant change. In More's account, he had been discussing making the king Pope, Supreme Head over all the Christian Church; Rich made this specific to the king's headship of the English Church and made More's refusal to acknowledge it patently foreign. Nevertheless, Rich suggested that More had not crossed any line into treason, reporting that he had ended their conversation by suggesting to the elder lawyer that 'your concealment to the question that hath been asked of you is as high offence as other that hath denied it.'[44] More, as far as Rich was concerned, had continued to successfully avoid declaring his mind on the matter, though Rich thought his silence should be prosecuted all the same.

More was interrogated further but refused to answer the questions on either the supremacy or the succession. On 22 June John Fisher was executed for his malicious denial of the king's supremacy. Three days later, a writ from the king declared that not only was Fisher a traitor, but so was Thomas More. Subjects were ordered to 'detest and abhor in their hearts' More's 'traitorous abuses and behaviours'. The timing of the writ, more than a week before More's trial, made its outcome inevitable. The king had already declared Thomas More a traitor and commanded all subjects to recognize the same.[45]

At More's trial on 1 July 1535, he was formally charged with 'high treason under the Act of Treasons concerning the Supremacy of the English Church'. There were three parts to the charge, all to do with his denial of the king's title of Supreme Head of the Church of England: 'maliciously remaining silent when asked to affirm it', 'maliciously conspiring with Bishop Fisher to deny the title' and 'maliciously asserting to Richard Rich that Parliament did not have power to grant the king this title'.

On the first charge, More held to the legal precedent of *qui tacet consentire videtur* and promised that 'my conscience had not been opened up to any mortal.' On the second, he maintained that any letters sent to Fisher during their mutual imprisonment had contained nothing more than 'familiar matters, such as our old custom and friendship called for', and so 'there is nothing on their account that should be judged worthy of death under your statute.' As More had legal precedent on his side and his letters to Fisher had been burned, there was little the judges could do to present evidence on these two counts.

The only evidence presented during the trial was the testimony offered by Rich on the third count. Clearly, he had changed his mind on his view of their discussion (likely with Cromwell's encouragement). He presented it to the court devoid of the framing of hypothetical 'putting of cases'; Rich asserted that More had stated outright that one 'cannot give his consent' to the case of the supremacy because Parliament could not 'make the king Supreme Head of the Church'. More responded with his own account, making clear he had been talking about the role of Pontiff, not head of the Church of England. What's more, as Roper related, More tried to explain that the conversation was 'familiar secret talk' and 'only in putting of cases', and thus not 'to be spoken maliciously'. And, 'where there is no malice, there can be no offense.'

Rich's testimony stood, however, and after a deliberation of only fifteen minutes, the jurors returned a guilty verdict. Between the verdict and the sentencing, More interrupted proceedings in order to declare his reasons for denying the king's supremacy at last. And it was the supremacy and not the succession to which he objected, though as all were aware the one depended on the other. His reasons, as he expressed them at his trial, were twofold: first, that no layman could become head of an ecclesiastical order; and second, that Henry's headship of the English Church represented a division within the Universal Church, requiring the consent of the rest of the Church, which Parliament did not have.

More was executed less than a week later, on 6 July 1535. His last words were recorded as being 'I die the king's good servant, and God's first,' a reference to the promise he held that the king had made to him on his entry into his service, and the jurisdictional priorities he had upheld in the final year of his life.

More was arrested for refusing to swear an oath upholding the Act of Succession, though he was executed for his denial of the king's supremacy. He had made clear that he would agree to swear simply to the rearrangement of the succession. His request, however, was denied – ostensibly by the king himself – who saw the two issues as irrevocably intertwined. He was not wrong. It would have been very difficult given the sequence of events to hold that the king could override the pope's dispensation, allowing his marriage to Catherine of Aragon, but not that he and not the pope was Supreme Head of the Church in England.

That being said, in More's view, the issue might not have been so convoluted. The statutes that More was being asked to recognize – first the succession and then the supremacy – were passed by Parliament. The real legal question around the succession was whether Parliament, not the king, had the right to declare Anne Boleyn queen of England and her daughter with Henry, Elizabeth, heir, in place of Catherine of Aragon and Mary. More would have held that neither king nor Parliament had the right to dissolve the king's marriage to Catherine and overturn the pope's dispensation. But his willingness to recognize the succession suggests that he saw this under the purview of Parliament's control and that he would have acknowledged the choosing of the monarch as a parliamentary power (akin to his arguments about the consent of the people legitimizing monarchs). The matter of the marriage or the associated issue of the king's supremacy needn't come into it for More. The two issues could be disentangled by focusing on Parliament's powers, not the king's.

If Henry realized that this was More's tack (and there's evidence that Cranmer and Cromwell did, if not the king), no wonder he reacted so strongly against Cranmer's suggestion that More be offered an oath simply on the succession. Significant power was granted to Parliament in the 1530s; acknowledging that it could independently decide the succession and (at least) the consort of England was not something Henry VIII would have happily tolerated. The entangling of the issues of the succession and the supremacy, then, was required to protect a sense of the king's authority in proceedings.

More hid his objections to the supremacy throughout the fifteen months of his imprisonment, though he did admit that he considered the act contrary to the laws of God. His Tower works reflect his prioritizing of spiritual obedience over temporal and a bolstering of his resolve in the face of persecution, imprisonment and death. His spiritual models are the martyrs of scripture as well as Christ himself, and his strategy of silence is drawn from his reading of the Psalms. It is also consistent, however, with his understanding of the law, and More is convinced by the rectitude of his approach in the eyes of both God and the courts. The coming together of God's law and legal jurisdictions are what makes More so firm in his position through his multiple interrogations and at his trial. The succession can be considered lawful as it contravenes the laws neither of God nor of man. The supremacy simply cannot. For that view, More died.

Epilogue

Responding to a history that he saw as irredeemably biased, Thomas More wrote, 'Let historians begin to show either prejudice or favouritism, and who will there be to lend any credence at all to histories?'[1] More's own literary and historical afterlife has been plagued by precisely such partialities, both favouritism and a desire to condemn, caught up as it has been in the vicissitudes of religious conflict, political ideologies and the popular dramatization of the Tudor court.

This began during his own life, as More was aware. He was forced to respond in his *Apology* to accusations that he had tortured Lutherans in his own home at Chelsea, and fiercely (though not absolutely) denied them. More's Europe-wide reputation was one of the reasons that he, in the eyes of Henry VIII and Thomas Cromwell, had to die. When Thomas Cranmer, Archbishop of Canterbury, suggested that More – and his colleague and friend John Fisher – might be allowed to take an oath to the Act of Succession, but not to the supremacy, Cromwell passed on the king's indignation and refusal; this would be a sign to the world that Henry VIII was not indeed Supreme Head of the Church in England. More's submission must be absolute, as Christendom watched.

It was very soon after his death that two literary Mores emerged. The first was from his own family and their allies, who faced persecution as traitors and Catholics in the latter years of the reign of Henry VIII and especially under his son, Edward VI. More's son-in-law, William Roper, composed a life of More, which went on to inform other lives produced by his circle. These were increasingly hagiographical accounts; the biography by More's great-grandson, Cresacre More, spoke of his ancestor's miracles, even as a baby.

> Shortly after his birth God would show by another sign, how dear this babe was unto him: For his nurse chancing to ride with him over a water, and her horse stepping aside into a deep place put both her and the child in great jeopardy; whose harms she seeking suddenly to prevent, threw the infant over a hedge into a field near adjoining . . . when she came to take him up again, she found him to have no hurt at all, but sweetly smiled upon her, that it might well be said of him 'Angelis suis Deus mandavit de te, ne te forte offendas ad lapidem pedem tuum;'[2] and not his foot only but his whole body.[3]

Paired with the publication of More's *Workes* under the Catholic Queen Mary I, these were explicit attempts to legitimize the growing cult around More and campaign for canonization from the pope.

Just as this saintly image of More was bolstered by the Catholic reign of Mary I, so too did the increasingly anti-Catholic reign of her sister, Elizabeth I, see the popularization of the rumours of More as violent Protestant-hunter. In his *Acts and Monuments*, John Foxe presents More as sadistic, cruel and decidedly *un*godly. After 1571 his 'Book of Martyrs', as it came to be known, was ordered by the crown to be placed in every cathedral church across England, cementing this view of More in the minds of God's people.[4]

Marcus Gheeraerts the Younger (attrib.), *William Cecil, Lord Burleigh*, after 1585, oil on panel.

Joining these religiously motivated presentations of More were others. His *Utopia* was translated into multiple European vernaculars through the sixteenth century, including English. The English *Utopia* was not a result of the More circle, who seemed inclined to disregard the work and did not include it in the 1557 *Workes*, but rather emerged first in the reign of Edward VI in 1551, with a second edition under Mary I, in 1556. Its translator, a goldsmith named Ralph Robinson, set the tone for a Protestant acceptance of *Utopia*, by attaching it to a proto-Protestant inclination of More that he later betrayed (which is why it might have been left out of the pro-Catholic *Workes*):

> This only I say, that it is much to be lamented of all, and not only of us his English men, that a man of so comparable wit, of so profound learning, and of so fine eloquence was yet nevertheless so much blinded, rather with obstinacy, than with ignorance, that he could not or rather would not see the shining light of God's holy truth in certain principle points of Christian religion, but did rather choose to persevere and continue in his wilful and stubborn obstinacy even to the very death.[5]

This attempt to separate the scholar More of *Utopia* – associated with Protestantism – from his unscholarly attachment to Catholic superstition was picked up in later centuries, including by David Hume in his *History of England*.

The word 'Utopia' had acquired a political purchase by the end of the sixteenth century, if not earlier. William Cecil, 1st Baron Burleigh (1520–1598), scrawled 'Utopia' in the margin of a document submitted by Hugh O'Neill during the Nine Years War (1594–1603), when his armies sought to expel the English, demanding the right of Ireland to effectively govern itself and practise whatever religion the people desired (that is, Catholicism).[6]

Burleigh, who had been the dedicatee of Ralph Robinson's translation in 1551, clearly knew what he meant, that such plans were a fantasy with no chance of being implemented, a usage that has survived to this day. As the *Oxford English Dictionary* notes, the adjective 'Utopian' was first used in a 'chiefly disparaging' manner, connoting 'a vision, plan, etc.: expressing or founded on an unrealistic belief in the perfectibility of society; excessively idealistic; impracticable; (of an ideal condition) illusory, unattainable'.[7] The flurry of 'dystopian' novels published in the wake of late nineteenth-century scientific advances and the horrific events of the twentieth century, such as E. M. Forster's *The Machine Stops* (1909), Yevgeny Zamyatin's *We* (1924), Aldous Huxley's *Brave New World* (1932) and George Orwell's *Animal Farm* (1945) and *Nineteen Eighty-Four* (1949) are all complicated and varied responses to what the authors see as a misguided attempt to implement Utopian social perfection. Similar responses are taking place now, especially in relation to the issues raised by Artificial Intelligence, with the widespread fear that the search for perfection will backfire, as Nick Bostrom explores in *Deep Utopia: Life and Meaning in a Solved World* (2024).

More's reputation was also that of a jester, a man able to crack jokes in the most trying of circumstances, as well as having the ability to calm down and unite antagonistic crowds. Edward Hall's *Chronicle* of 1548 reports on More's scaffold jokes – 'he desired one of the Sheriff's officers to give him his hand to help him up, and said, when I come down again, let me shift for myself as well as I can' – and he cannot decide whether More is 'a foolish wiseman or a wise foolishman', a presentation that persists in other chronicles of the age.[8]

These qualities are evident in the Elizabethan play *Sir Thomas More* (*c.* 1591–3), a collaborative work, most likely by Henry Chettle (d. 1603–7) and Anthony Munday (*c.* 1560–1633) for the Rose Theatre, which survives only in manuscript and was probably never performed on stage, perhaps because it was thought to have Catholic sympathies. The play has attracted attention because the manuscript contains revisions in a hand many have identified as that of Shakespeare.

The play follows events in the life of More from his intervention to stop the aggressive xenophobic crowd during the 'Evil May Day' riots (1 May 1517), when foreign apprentices and workers were set upon by an enraged London mob, to his execution. The action is centred, like several other plays in the 1590s, on the citizens of London. Henry VIII does not appear and the reason for More's execution is not made clear, presumably because it was so well known and it would have been provocative to represent the issue given the careful censorship of religious material on the stage. The play is therefore a distorted story of More's life, casting him as a 'merry man', wise, friendly and popular with ordinary people, at ease with himself and the world, prepared for whatever fate comes his way.

The authorities are shown to be inept in their plans to quell and disperse the angry crowd, until More takes control and demonstrates his ability to communicate with the common people. When an enraged shopkeeper, George, tells More that they plan to expel the 'strangers' who are threatening their livelihood, More confronts them with the malign consequences of their actions:

> Grant them removed, and grant that this your noise
> Hath chid down all the majesty of England.
> Imagine that you see the wretched strangers,
> Their babies at their backs, and their poor luggage
> Plodding to th' ports and coasts for transportation,
> And that you sit as kings in your desires,
> Authority quite silent by your brawl,
> And you in ruff of your opinions clothed:
> What had you got? I'll tell you: you had taught

> How insolence and strong hand should prevail,
> How order should be quelled; and by this pattern
> Not one of you should live an aged man,
> For other ruffians, as their fancies wrought,
> With selfsame hand, self reasons, and self right
> Would shark on you, and men like ravenous fishes
> Would feed on one another.[9]

More's speech works effectively to quieten the hostile crowd. It is a skilful piece of rhetoric, appealing to the humanity of those assembled and their sympathy for others from the same social class, so that they are imagined as equals and workers rather than immigrants competing for resources. More is seen as a man of the people, reminding the London citizens that they are fair-minded and reasonable and that they need to think about the future consequences of their actions. More warns them that if they turn against the foreign workers, they will break down authority and so make life more unfair and anarchic, paving the way for 'other ruffians' to bully them in turn, as law and order disappear, and justice is replaced by the rule of the strongest. While the citizens are hostile to the authorities that rule them, if they refuse to obey established laws they will become what they despise, sitting as kings dressed in finery and lording it over those they are able to bully. The speech contains dangerous sentiments, suggesting that the common people and their masters should always be at odds, and that they must unite with those of the same social stratum regardless of origin. Whether we are to take its message at face value and see it as a piece of wisdom uttered by the man acknowledged to be the wisest man in England, or view it as a cunning strategy by someone who knows how to deal with extreme situations, is not made clear in the play. Either way, it works well, the audience declaring that More's words are 'as true as the gospel' and that the speaker is 'a sound fellow'.[10]

When brought to his place of execution More jokes in the face of death, remarking to the sheriff when he sees the scaffold that he has 'come about a headless errant', punning on his imminent beheading and pretending that he has forgotten why he is where he is.[11] He continues the joke, as he turns to the sympathetic sheriff leading him to his death:

In troth, methinks, your stair is somewhat weak:
I prithee, honest friend, lend me thy hand
To help me up. As for my coming down,
Let me alone, I'll look to that myself.[12]

More is shown to be fearless and eager to ease any pain others might feel about his execution, a man who is secure in his faith and sense of himself and who uses his wit and intelligence for the benefit of others (as he did when dealing with the potential rioters). The execution scene continues with More's good sense and good humour continuing. He praises the king ('I confess his majesty hath been ever good to me')[13] and blames himself for his fate, the normal requirement of a proper scaffold speech.[14] When the hangman asks More to forgive him for his death, More replies that it should be the other way round as he has caused the hangman's discomfort through his need to administer the harshest penalty of the law, and he pays him his fee and jokes that his beard was cut off (executed) the previous night. He concludes, however, with words of sententious wisdom:

We go to sigh; that o'er, to sleep in rest.
Here More forsakes all mirth; good reason why:
The fool of flesh must with her frail life die.
No eye salute my trunk with a sad tear:
Our birth to heaven should be thus: void of fear.[15]

A good life is concluded by a good death.

There are few significant changes to More's legacy in the centuries that followed. In the eighteenth and nineteenth centuries, *Utopia* – and by extension its author – was claimed by various emerging ideological camps, perhaps most notably communists, led by Marx and Engels. Though the pair condemned 'utopian

Thomas More listed among the heroes of the Communist Revolution on the Romanov Obelisk, Moscow.

socialism', they were admirers of More's work, and placed him as the first writer of the communist movement, at least in England. Their copy of *Utopia* – the Robinson edition, prized as a 'popular' edition – shows thorough reading, and the famous passage about man-eating sheep, quoted by Marx, is underlined.

The twentieth century saw the revival of attempts to canonize More, which bore fruit in 1935, on the quatercentenary of his death. There were many reasons for this return to More as an English Catholic figure. One *Times* correspondent reported from the Vatican that it was intended as a 'hint to Herr Hitler', 'showing the light in which the Vatican regards those German Roman Catholics who have been done to death by Nazi extremists'.[16]

Stained glass of Thomas More at St Dunstan's Church, Canterbury.

More's canonization was accompanied by a new biography, produced by the Catholic scholar R. W. Chambers. This drew almost exclusively on the hagiographical accounts of More and presents him unequivocally as a saintly scholar, as well as a hero of European civilization:

> to depict More not only as a martyr (which he was) but also a great European statesman; More's far-sighted outlook was neglected amid the selfish despotisms of his age; yet his words, his acts, and his sufferings were consistently, through life, based upon principles which have survived him. More was killed, but these principles must, in the end, triumph. If they do not, the civilization of Europe is doomed.[17]

Chambers's biography inspired perhaps the most influential presentation of More, as the central character in Robert Bolt's *Man for All Seasons*, first produced as a play in 1960, and then as an Oscar-winning film in 1966. Bolt's More is both saintly and scholarly, to be sure, as well as witty and fatherly, but he also introduces a new – and entirely ahistorical – element to the character, investing More with a passionate individualism characteristic of the 1960s anti-war and anti-nuclear movements of which Bolt was a part. Paul Scofield famously delivers the line in the film, 'But what matters to me is not whether it's true or not, but that I believe it to be true, or rather not that I *believe* it, but that *I* believe it.' Bolt's More stands against the oppressive power of the state to quash individual belief, a view completely at odds with the historical More, whose objections were rooted in his participation with a *larger* majority than the state, rather than the defence of a minority view against it. Bolt's representation of More transforms him from a committed religious figure to a modern existential hero challenging the power of the state.

In response to what he identified as a 'cloying, unrelenting, often unthinking defense of More', Richard Marius produced his 1983 biography of the man, which took up the Foxean sources and attempted to psychoanalyse More's writings and actions, especially his persecution of Protestants.[18] The multilayered and conflicting accounts of More's life, combined with a dearth in primary sources, caused the Tudor historian and More scholar John Guy to declare in 2000 that 'a truly historical biography of More' was impossible.[19] This challenge was taken up 25 years later by Joanne Paul, whose biography seeks 'to work "forward" from the contemporary sources' and not '"backward" from those that followed his death', and thus to present a more holistic picture of More.[20]

The celebration of William Tyndale in modern Protestant religious and intellectual circles, in the United Kingdom and United States in particular, has further caused a backlash against the image of the saintly Thomas More, especially after the publication of David Daniell's widely read biography of 1994.[21]

Paul Scofield as Thomas More in *A Man for All Seasons* (1966).

Tyndale is celebrated as the first proper translator of the Bible into English, murdered by the reactionary Catholic forces who stymied the progress of the Reformation after the execution of Anne Boleyn. More is sometimes accused of direct involvement in the kidnap and execution of Tyndale, but more often excoriated as his most heated and bitter opponent, a man who was desperate not to let the ordinary people read the Bible they desperately wanted and eager to uphold the reactionary power of the Catholic Church.

More as repressed religious zealot too found a dramatic manifestation, in Hilary Mantel's lauded novel *Wolf Hall* (2009), which was produced as a six-episode television series in 2015. Guy described Mantel's More as 'a sneering, conceited, misogynist bigot of the worst sort, a pantomime villain born with a spoon in his mouth', and Mantel herself wrote in an imagined

Anton Lesser as Thomas More in *Wolf Hall* (2015).

letter to More that 'we have to lie about you a little in order to like you.'[22] *Wolf Hall* was unabashed in its presentation of More as a zealous murderer of Protestants, leading to suggestions that More was comparable to the extremist Islamic State.[23] The rise of Thomas Cromwell, represented as a capable, brilliant and talented man oppressed by his role in the gruesome affairs of state, has come at the expense of Thomas More. It seems that popular perceptions of the reign of Henry VIII have been forced to choose one hero either between More and Tyndale, or between Cromwell and More.

The quincentenary of the publication of *Utopia* in 2016 resulted in a series of reassessments of the text and its legacy, which included the revival of not only the notion that *Utopia* was a precursor to twentieth-century totalitarianism, but utopian thinking as a means to combat the growing climate emergency. *Utopia*, however, at least in scholarly treatments often remains distanced from More's wider biographical reputation, leading many to adhere to – and decry – the 'multiple Mores thesis': the idea that distinct 'Mores' can be identified and treated, due to the opposition present in his life and works.

This, too, has been challenged by historians who identify through-lines in More's work, and advocate for the reading of More's entire oeuvre. The twenty-first century has seen a renewed attempt to recover a holistic and historical view of More as a complex figure, rightly so given the relatively easy access readers now have to his works, and the ready availability of large selections from them. As Mantel told her fictional More, sounding very much like the man himself, 'Liking you, disliking you, it shouldn't matter – not to sober historians.'[24] More will surely always be a controversial and divisive figure, his life well documented, his voluminous writings available, the subject of both comment and analysis from the immediate aftermath of his execution onwards. There is always room for yet more interpretation. This enigmatic, discussion-provoking More is very much the creation of his own writings, and perhaps intentionally so. The 'real' More does not need to be one that can be fully and finally defined.

Statue of Thomas More by L. Cubitt Bevis, erected 1969, Chelsea, London.

CHRONOLOGY

1478 Thomas More born in London
1485 Begins formal schooling at St Anthony's Threadneedle Street
1489 Enters the household of the Lord Chancellor and Archbishop of Canterbury, John Morton
1492 Becomes a student at Oxford
1494 Returns to London and becomes a student of the law
1499 Meets Erasmus, as well as the future King Henry VIII
1506 Publishes translations of Lucian with Erasmus
1510 Publishes *Life of Pico*
1513 Begins writing *History of King Richard III*
1515 Begins writing *Utopia*; writes 'Letter to Dorp'
1516 *Utopia* published at Leuven
1518 Becomes a privy councillor to Henry VIII; third edition of *Utopia* is published at Basel, along with the Latin poems
1519 Writes 'Letter to a Monk' and 'Letter to Lee'
1522 Writes *The Four Last Things*
1523 Publishes the *Response to Luther*
1529 Publishes *A Dialogue Concerning Heresies* and *The Supplication of Souls*; becomes Lord Chancellor
1532 Publishes the first part of *The Confutation of Tyndale's Answer* and 'Letter Against Frith'; resigns as Lord Chancellor
1533 Publishes the second part of *The Confutation of Tyndale's Answer*, *The Apology of Thomas More*, *Debellation of Salem and Bizance* and *The Answer to a Poisoned Book*
1534 Writes *A Treatise to Receive the Blessed Body*, *A Treatise on the Passion* and *A Dialogue of Comfort Against Tribulation*
1535 Writes *On the Sadness of Christ*; tried, convicted and executed for treason

REFERENCES

Abbreviations

BAJ	*British Art Journal*
BL	British Library
CTM	*The Correspondence of Thomas More*, ed. Elizabeth Frances Rogers (New Haven, CT, 1947)
CW	*The Complete Works of St Thomas More*, ed. Louis L. Martz et al., 15 vols (New Haven, CT, 1962–97)
CWE	*The Collected Works of Erasmus* (Toronto, 1975–)
ES	*Erasmus Studies*
HJ	*Historical Journal*
JBS	*Journal of British Studies*
JEH	*Journal of Ecclesiastical History*
JTS	*Journal of Theological Studies*
LC	*Literature Compass*
LJ	*London Journal*
LMA	London Metropolitan Archives
ODNB	*Oxford Dictionary of National Biography* (www.oxforddnb.com)
ORE	*Oxford Research Encyclopedias* (https://oxfordre.com)
P. & P.	*Past and Present*
RS	*Renaissance Studies*
SL	*Thomas More: Selected Letters*, ed. Elizabeth Frances Rogers (New Haven, CT, 1961)
Tilley	Maurice Palmer Tilley, *A Dictionary of the Proverbs in England in the Sixteenth and Seventeenth Centuries: A Collection of the Proverbs Found in English Literature and the Dictionaries of the Period* (Ann Arbor, MI, 1950)
TNA	The National Archives
TRHS	*Transactions of the Royal Historical Society*
YULG	*Yale University Library Gazette*

Introduction

1 For further reflections on this issue see Andrew Hadfield, 'Why Does Literary Biography Matter?', *Shakespeare Quarterly*, LXV/4 (2015), pp. 371–8.
2 Readers should consult Joanne Paul, *Thomas More: A Life and Death in Tudor England* (Harmondsworth, 2025).
3 Frank Mitjans, *Thomas More's Vocation* (Washington, DC, 2023), p. 266.
4 For More's birthdate see Frank Mitjans, 'The Date of Birth of Thomas More', *Moreana*, XLVII/181–2 (2010), pp. 109–28, and Frank Mitjans, 'Reviewing and Correcting the Article on the Date of Birth of Thomas More', *Moreana*, XLIX/189–90 (2012), pp. 251–62. Recent work has suggested he was not born on Milk Street, as has commonly been held, but in the parish of St Giles without Cripplegate; see Joanne Paul, 'The Milk Street Mystery: Thomas More's Birthplace', *Moreana*, LXI/1 (2024), pp. 76–86.
5 Caroline M. Barron, 'The Making of a London Citizen', in *The Cambridge Companion to Thomas More*, ed. George M. Logan, Cambridge Companions to Religion (Cambridge, 2011), pp. 3–21.
6 CW, vol. XV, p. 25 ('Letter to Dorp').
7 Joanne Paul, 'The More–Morton Connection: How Thomas More Came to Be at Lambeth Palace', *Moreana*, LXII/1 (2025), pp. 87–93.
8 CW, vol. III, pt 2, pp. 295, 297, nos 273, 295.
9 W. A. Pantin, *Canterbury College*, vol. IV (Oxford, 1985), pp. 56, 85–91; Barron, 'Making of a London Citizen', p. 10.
10 CW, vol. XV, p. 139 ('Letter to the University of Oxford').
11 Pantin, *Canterbury College*, vol. IV, pp. 79, 82–3.
12 Ibid., pp. 99–100.
13 CW, vol. XV, p. 131 ('Letter to the University of Oxford').
14 CWE, vol. VII, p. 19.
15 Robert Megarry, *Inns Ancient and Modern: A Topographical and Historical Introduction to the Inns of Court, Inns of Chancery, and Serjeants' Inns* (London, 1989), ch. 3. More generally see J. H. Baker, 'The English Legal Profession 1450–1550', in *Collected Papers on English Legal History* (Cambridge, 2013), pp. 19–44.
16 Samuel E. Thorne and J. H. Baker, eds, *Readings and Moots at the Inns of Court in the Fifteenth Century*, vol. II (London, 1990), p. xvi.
17 Letter translated in Mitjans, *Vocation*, p. 33.
18 CWE, vol. VII, p. 2.
19 Anne F. Sutton, *The Mercery of London: Trade, Goods and People, 1130–1578* (London, 2005), p. 94.

20 TNA PROB 11/11/559, fol. 224.
21 *CTM*, p. 4.
22 CW, vol. I, p. 9.
23 *CWE*, vol. VII, p. 21.
24 CW, vol. III, pt 2, no. 143, p. 187.
25 TNA SC 6/HENVIII/2396.
26 CW, vol. XV, p. 23 ('Letter to Dorp').
27 Laetitia Lyell and Frank D. Watney, eds, *Acts of Court of the Mercers' Company, 1453–1527* (Cambridge, 2012), pp. 320–21.
28 LMA COL/CC/01/01/011, fol. 93r.
29 Jonathan McGovern, *The Tudor Sheriff: A Study in Early Modern Administration* (Oxford, 2022), p. 71; Jonathan McGovern, 'The Compters at Poultry and Wood Street in Early Modern London', *LJ*, XLVI/3 (2 September 2021), pp. 249–67 (p. 251).
30 See Mitjans, *Vocation*, pp. 72, 78, 121–3. Mitjans, based on the evidence in later biographies, suggests that More translated the *Life of Pico* in 1505; the later *Works of Thomas More*, published by William Rastell, suggest it was translated about 1510.
31 John Guy, *A Daughter's Love* (London, 2008), p. 47.
32 A. W. Reed, *Early Tudor Drama: Medwall, the Rastells, Heywood, and the More Circle* (London, 1926), p. 7.
33 Guy, *Daughter's Love*, pp. 49–50; Steven Gunn, *Charles Brandon: Henry VIII's Closest Friend* (Stroud, 2015), p. 35.
34 CW, vol. XV, p. 49.
35 *CWE*, vol. III, no. 388, p. 235.
36 *CTM*, no. 199, p. 495.
37 *CWE*, vol. V, no. 784.
38 CW, vol. XV, p. 263 ('Letter to a Monk').
39 *SL*, no. 53, p. 212.
40 Elizabeth McCutcheon, 'Margaret More Roper: The Learned Woman in Tudor England', *Moreana*, LII/201–2 (2015), pp. 269–97 (p. 272); Elizabeth McCutcheon, 'The Education of Thomas More's Daughters: Concepts and Praxis I', *Moreana*, LII/201–2 (2015), pp. 249–68 (pp. 254–5).
41 Judith P. Jones and Sherianne Sellers Seibel, 'Thomas More's Feminism: To Reform or Re-Form', *Albion: A Quarterly Journal Concerned with British Studies*, X (Quincentennial Essays on St Thomas More) (1978), pp. 67–77 (p. 68).
42 *SL*, no. 20, p. 105.
43 *CWE*, vol. VIII, no. 1233, p. 297.

44 Martin Luther, *Contra Henricvm, regem Angliae*, 1522; Martin Luther, *Contra Henricum Regem Angliae*, ed. E. S. Buchanan (New York, 1928), available at http://anglicanhistory.org.
45 See David Colclough, *Freedom of Speech in Early Stuart England* (Cambridge, 2005), pp. 31–4.
46 CW, vol. IV, p. 125.
47 'Landownership: More's Estate', in *A History of the County of Middlesex*, vol. XII: *Chelsea*, ed. Patricia E. C. Croot (London, 2004), pp. 115–18; Guy, *Daughter's Love*, p. 147.
48 Xavier F. Salomon, 'Holbein's Sir Thomas More', in Hilary Mantel and Xavier F. Salomon, *Holbein's Sir Thomas More* (New York, 2018), pp. 9–66.
49 Alexander Marr, 'Holbein's Earliest Portraits in England? The Sequence of His Work for Sir Thomas More', *BAJ*, XXIV/3 (2023), pp. 49–57.
50 *SL*, no. 199, pp. 207–8.
51 Quoted in John Guy and Julia Fox, *Hunting the Falcon: Henry VIII, Anne Boleyn and the Marriage That Shook Europe*, 1st edn (London, 2023), p. 76.
52 G. W. Bernard, 'The Fall of Wolsey Reconsidered', *JBS*, XXXV/3 (1996), pp. 277–310 (p. 277).
53 *CTM*, no. 199, p. 495.
54 P. J. Holmes, 'The Last Tudor Great Councils', *HJ*, XXXIII/1 (1990), pp. 1–22 (p. 8).
55 *CTM*, no. 199, p. 496; no. 208, p. 534.
56 G. R. Elton, 'More and the Opposition to Henry VIII', *Moreana*, IV/15–16, 3–4 (1967), pp. 285–303 (p. 288).
57 Guy, *Daughter's Love*, pp. 196–7; Elton, 'More', p. 289.
58 CW, vol. IX, p. 126 (*Apology*).
59 Stanford E. Lehmberg, *The Reformation Parliament, 1529–1536* (Cambridge, 1970), p. 15.
60 Quoted ibid., p. 115.
61 Ibid., pp. 149–50; Michael Kelly, 'The Submission of the Clergy', *TRHS*, XV (1965), pp. 97–119 (p. 112).
62 G. R. Elton, '1. The Law of Treason in the Early Reformation', *HJ*, XI/2 (1968), pp. 211–36 (p. 231).

1 Early Humanist Writings

1 James McConica, 'Thomas More as Humanist', in *The Cambridge Companion to Thomas More*, ed. George M. Logan (Cambridge, 2011),

pp. 22–45; Paul Oskar Kristeller, 'Thomas More as a Renaissance Humanist', *Moreana*, XVII/65–6 (1980), pp. 5–22.

2 On humanism see Margaret L. King, ed. and trans., *Renaissance Humanism: An Anthology of Sources* (Indianapolis, IN, 2014); and Donald R. Kelley, *Renaissance Humanism* (New York, 1991).

3 On Christian humanism see Brendan Bradshaw, 'The Christian Humanism of Erasmus', *JTS*, XXXIII/2 (1982), pp. 411–47.

4 Walter Nicgorski, 'More's *Utopia*: Between and Beyond Plato and Cicero', *Moreana*, LIV/2 (2017), pp. 129–40.

5 Micha Lazarus, 'Greek Literacy in Sixteenth-Century England', *RS*, XXIX/3 (2015), pp. 433–58.

6 See John Guy, *The Public Career of Sir Thomas More* (New Haven, CT, 1977).

7 CW, vol. III, introduction, p. xliii.

8 Cesare Vasoli, 'The Renaissance Concept of Philosophy', in *The Cambridge History of Renaissance Philosophy*, ed. Charles B. Schmitt and Quentin Skinner (Cambridge, 1988), pp. 57–74 (pp. 68–70).

9 CW, vol. I, p. 70.

10 CW, vol. III, pt 2, pp. 84–5.

11 Ibid., pp. 88–9.

12 'While Tyndarus happened to be kissing a girl whose outstanding characteristic was not the smallness of her nose, he felt a sudden impulse to be witty about it. Said he, "I cannot make my lips reach yours, for your nose keeps my mouth at a distance." The girl immediately blushed and burned with repressed anger, stung by his not very witty witticism. "If my nose keeps your kisses from my mouth," she said, "then you can kiss me here, where I have no nose"' (CW, vol. III, p. 219, epigram 187).

13 CW, vol. III, pt 2, pp. 134–5.

14 Ibid., pp. 230–31.

15 Gerard Wegemer, 'Thomas More on Tyranny: What Is Distinctive in His Early Thematic and Literary Treatment?', *Moreana*, XLIX/1 (2012), pp. 41–56; John Guy, 'More and Tyranny', *Moreana*, XLIX/1 (2012), pp. 57–88.

16 CW, vol. III, pt 2, pp. 144–5.

17 Ibid., pp. 210–11.

18 Ibid., pp. 144–5.

19 CW, vol. I, p. 354.

20 Ibid., p. 3.

21 Ibid.

22 Tracey Hill, 'Festivals', in *The Ashgate Research Companion to Popular Culture in Early Modern England*, ed. Matthew Dimmock, Andrew Hadfield and Abigail Shinn (Farnham, 2014), pp. 43–58.
23 CW, vol. I, introduction, p. xxvi.
24 'When a hatter will go to think in philosophy, or a peddler becomes a meddler in theology, all that follows [is that] they drive such new skills so far astray, they in this way cause misfortune on themselves' (CW, vol. I, p. 16, ll. 54–62).
25 John Skelton, 'Elynour Rummynge', in *The Complete English Poems*, ed. John Scattergood (Harmondsworth, 1983), ll. 12–21.
26 Ibid., ll. 368–80.
27 Ibid., ll. 387–82.
28 Ibid., ll. 428–9.
29 CW, vol. I, p. 46.
30 Sir Thomas Wyatt, 'They Flee from Me', in *The Complete Poems*, ed. R. A. Rebholz (Harmondsworth, 1978), pp. 116–17.
31 Susan Brigden, *Thomas Wyatt: The Heart's Forest* (London, 2012), pp. 149–50.
32 CW, vol. V, p. 176.
33 CW, vol. II, p. 81.
34 See Alison Hanham, 'The Texts of Thomas More's *Richard III*', RS, XXI/1 (2007), pp. 62–84.
35 CW, vol. 3, pt 2, no. 188, p. 221. These *Epigrams* were published alongside *Utopia* in 1518.
36 CW, vol. II, p. 83.
37 Ibid., p. 12.
38 Ibid., p. 6.
39 CW, vol. III, pt I, pp. 108, 95.
40 Ibid., pt 2, no. 121, p. 169.
41 CW, vol. I, p. lxiv.
42 On medieval eschatological sermons see Thom Mertens et al., eds, *The Last Judgement in Medieval Preaching* (Turnhout, 2013).
43 CW, vol. I, p. 146.
44 Ibid., p. 172.

2 More and Erasmus

1 Robert Kolb, 'The Debate between Martin Luther and Erasmus', ORE, 29 March 2017, https://doi.org/10.1093/acrefore/9780199340378.013.505.

2 CWE, vol. VII, pp. 17–18.
3 Lisa Jardine, *Erasmus, Man of Letters: The Construction of Charisma in Print* (Princeton, NJ, 1993).
4 Christopher Marlow, 'Friendship in Renaissance England', LC, 15 December 2005, https://doi.org/10.1111/j.1741-4113.2004.00011.x.
5 It is worth noting, however, that while publicly – and perhaps privately – Erasmus condemned More's service at the court, Erasmus never let up seeking a paid post in England and the patronage of men like Cardinal Wolsey: see Cecil H. Clough, 'Erasmus and the Pursuit of English Royal Patronage in 1517 and 1518', ES, 1 (1981), pp. 126–40.
6 On the composition see CWE, vol. VII, p. 83.
7 CWE, vol. XXVIII, introduction, p. xx.
8 CWE, vol. XXVII, p. 83.
9 Arthur F. Kinney, *Humanist Poetics: Thought, Rhetoric and Fiction in Sixteenth-Century England* (Amherst, 1988), ch. 2.
10 Margot Johnson, 'Ruthall, Thomas', ODNB online.
11 CW, vol. III, pt 2, pp. 3–5.
12 Ibid., p. 5.
13 CW, vol. III, p. 196.
14 CWE, vol. V, pp. 7–8.
15 Ibid., pp. 52–3.
16 See Joanne Paul, *Counsel and Command in Early Modern English Thought* (Cambridge, 2020).
17 For the history of the exchange see Sister M. Scholastica Cooper, 'More and the Letter to Martin Dorp', *Moreana*, VI/2 (1965), pp. 37–44.
18 CW, vol. XV, pp. 9–11.
19 Ibid., p. 107.
20 Ibid., p. 109.
21 Ibid., p. 123.
22 Ibid., p. xlii.
23 Ibid., p. 201.
24 Ibid., p. 203.
25 Ibid., p. 209.
26 Ibid., p. 69. On the significance of Peter Lombard's *Sentences* see Philipp W. Rosemann, *The Story of a Great Medieval Book: Peter Lombard's 'Sentences'* (Ontario, 2007).
27 CW, vol. XV, p. 71.
28 Ibid., p. 71.
29 Ricardo J. Quinones, *Dualisms: The Agons of the Modern World* (Toronto, 2007), pp. 54–5.

30 CW, vol. XV, p. 271.
31 Ibid., p. 281.
32 Ibid., pp. 293–5.
33 CWE, vol. III, p. 230.
34 Ibid., p. 232.
35 Ibid., p. 234.
36 Ibid., p. 316.
37 CWE, vol. IV, p. 171.
38 Ibid., pp. 163–4.
39 Ibid., p. 368.
40 Andrew Hadfield, 'Travel', in *Cultural Reformations: Medieval and Renaissance in Literary History*, ed. Brian Cummings and James Simpson (Oxford, 2010), pp. 134–49 (p. 136).
41 CW, vol. XV, p. 190.

3 *Utopia*

1 More was unhappy with the Leuven edition. The Basel editions – March and November 1518 – also include his Latin epigrams.
2 J. H. Hexter, *More's Utopia: The Biography of an Idea* (New York, 1965).
3 Notre Dame, which became a cathedral in 1559.
4 Elizabeth McCutcheon, 'Thomas More, Raphael Hythlodaeus, and the Angel Raphael', *Moreana*, LII/201–2 (2015), pp. 16–36.
5 Patricia Parker, *Shakespeare from the Margins: Language, Culture, Context* (Chicago, IL, 1996), p. 275.
6 See Frank Mitjans, *Thomas More's Vocation* (Washington, DC, 2023).
7 CW, vol. IV, p. 55.
8 Ibid., p. 57.
9 Ibid., p. 97.
10 Ibid., p. 99.
11 Ibid., p. 101.
12 Ibid., p. 103.
13 Ibid., p. 103; Plato, *Republic*, 6.496 D–E.
14 CTM, no. 206, p. 519.
15 CW, vol. IV, p. 105.
16 Ibid., p. 245.
17 Quentin Skinner, 'Thomas More's *Utopia* and the Virtue of True Nobility', in *Visions of Politics*, vol. II: *Renaissance Virtues* (Cambridge, 2002), pp. 213–44.
18 CW, vol. IV, pp. 245–7.

19 CW, vol. IX, p. 167, our emphasis.
20 CW, vol. IV, pp. 185–7.
21 CW, vol. VII, pp. 179, 357.
22 CW, vol. VI, p. 327.
23 Ibid., p. 327.
24 CW, vol. VIII, pp. 503–5, 840–41.
25 CW, vol. IV, pp. 187–9.
26 Ibid., p. 189.
27 Ibid., p. 127.
28 Ibid., p. 131.
29 Ibid., p. 145.
30 Ibid., p. 137.
31 Ibid., p. 133.
32 See Matthew Dimmock and Andrew Hadfield, eds, *Amazons, Savages, and Machiavels: Travel and Colonial Writing in English, 1550–1630: An Anthology*, 2nd expanded edn (Oxford, 2022), pp. 125–32.
33 Philippe Contamine, *War in the Middle Ages*, trans. Michael Jones (Oxford, 1986).
34 See Andrew Hadfield, '*Utopia* and Travel Writing', in *The Oxford Handbook of More's 'Utopia'*, ed. Cathy Shrank and Phil Withington (Oxford, 2024), pp. 106–21.
35 Pablo Garcia and Kathleen Myers, 'Spanish Catholicism in the Era of Exploration and Early Colonization', in *The Cambridge History of Religions in America*, vol. I: *Pre-Columbian Times to 1790*, ed. Stephen J. Stein (Cambridge, 2000), pp. 177–99.
36 Eric Nelson, *The Greek Tradition in Republican Thought* (Cambridge, 2004), pp. 19–48.
37 CW, vol. VI, p. 185.
38 Ibid.
39 Ibid., p. 217.
40 Ibid.
41 Ibid., pp. 217–19.
42 Terence Cave, *Thomas More's 'Utopia' in Early Modern Europe: Paratexts and Contexts* (Manchester, 2008), ch. 1.
43 *SL*, no. 7, p. 76.
44 A poem and verse from John Desmarais was removed from the 1518 edition, along with another letter from More to Gillis.
45 CW, vol. VI, p. 3.
46 Ibid., p. 11.
47 *Udepotia* in the text.

48 CW, vol. VI, p. 21.
49 Ibid., p. 23.
50 Ibid., p. 41.
51 M. Bishop, 'Ambrosius Holbein's Memento Mori Map for Sir Thomas More's *Utopia*: The Meanings of a Masterpiece of Early Sixteenth Century Graphic Art', *British Dental Journal*, CXCIX/2 (July 2005), pp. 107–12; Joanne Paul, *Thomas More: A Life and Death in Tudor England* (London, 2025), p. 55.

4 Writing on Heresy

1 Eiléan Ni Chuilleanáin, in a sympathetic overview, acknowledges that many see these works as 'bitter, bullying, and, worst of all, tedious': 'The Debate between Thomas More and William Tyndale, 1528–33: Ideas on Literature and Religion', *JEH*, XXXIX/3 (1988), pp. 382–411 (p. 382).
2 C. S. Lewis, *English Literature in the Sixteenth Century Excluding Drama* (Oxford, 1954), pp. 171–2.
3 CW, vol. V, p. 7.
4 Genesis 11:1–9.
5 CW, vol. V, pp. 77–9.
6 Ibid., p. 103.
7 Ibid., p. 287.
8 Ibid., p. 239.
9 CW, vol. VIII, pt 1, p. 569.
10 CW, vol. VI, pp. 202–3.
11 On More and *The City of God* see M. N. Raitiere, 'More's Utopia and *The City of God*', *Studies in the Renaissance*, XX (1973), pp. 144–68.
12 CW, vol. VI, p. 123.
13 Angela Hobbs, 'More and the Republics of Plato', in *The Oxford Handbook of Thomas More's 'Utopia'*, ed. Cathy Shrank and Phil Withington (Oxford, 2023), pp. 19–35.
14 CW, vol. VI, p. 409.
15 See Eamon Duffy, *Fires of Faith: Catholic England under Mary Tudor* (New Haven, CT, 2009).
16 CW, vol. VII, p. 234.
17 Tilley, F286.
18 CW, vol. VII, p. 168.
19 See Victoria Flood, *Prophecy, Politics and Place in Medieval England: From Geoffrey of Monmouth to Thomas of Erceldoune* (Woodbridge, 2016).

20 CW, vol. VIII, pt 1, p. 275.
21 David Daniell, *The Bible in English: Its History and Influence* (New Haven, CT, 2003), p. 448.
22 CW, vol. VIII, pt 3, p. 1521.
23 Ibid., pt 1, p. 165.
24 Ibid., pt 2, p. 577.
25 Ibid.
26 Ibid., p. 627.
27 CW, vol. VI, p. 121.
28 Ibid., p. 166, our emphasis.
29 Ibid., p. 289.
30 Ibid.
31 Ibid., p. 290.
32 Brian Cummings, *The Literary Culture of the Reformation: Grammar and Grace* (Oxford, 2002).
33 Eamon Duffy, *The Stripping of the Altars: Traditional Religion in England, 1400–1580* (New Haven, CT, 1992); Eamon Duffy, *The Voices of Morebath: Reformation and Rebellion in an English Village* (New Haven, CT, 2001).
34 CW, vol. V, p. 395. As the editors of the edition point out, there is no precise biblical verse that states what More claims, but he is probably thinking of Ezekiel 33:12, Joel 2:32, Acts 2:21, Mark 16:16 and Romans 10:13.
35 CW, vol. V, p. 189.
36 CW, vol. XI, p. 173.
37 Ibid., p. 147.

5 Oath of Supremacy, Trial and Late Spiritual Writings

1 Jonathan Michael Gray, *Oaths and the English Reformation* (Cambridge, 2012), p. 82.
2 Elements of what follow are drawn from Joanne Paul, *Thomas More: A Life* (London, 2025), chs 18–20.
3 Diarmaid MacCulloch, *Thomas Cromwell: A Life* (London, 2018), p. 144.
4 Quoted in Stanford E. Lehmberg, *The Reformation Parliament, 1529–36* (Cambridge, 1970), p. 11.
5 See ibid., p. 115; MacCulloch, *Thomas Cromwell*, p. 147.
6 Haus-, Hof- und Stadtarchiv [Austrian State Archives], StAbt England Diplomatische Korr. Box 5 1531, no. 10 fols 19^{v}–20^{r}.

7 William Roper, *The Life of Sir Thomas More*, ed. Gerard Wegemer and Stephen W. Smith (Dallas, TX, 2003), p. 29, available at https://thomasmorestudies.org.
8 CW, vol. IX, p. 53.
9 Ibid., p. 54.
10 Frank Mitjans, *Thomas More's Vocation* (Washington, DC, 2023), p. 269.
11 Haus-, Hof- und Stadtarchiv, StAbt England Diplomatische Korr. Box 5 1532, no. 24, fol. 60r. More addressed rumours that he had been removed from office unwillingly in a letter to Erasmus; *SL*, no. 46, p. 179.
12 CW, vol. VIII, pt 2, pp. 576–7.
13 Ibid., pt 1, p. 146.
14 Ibid., pt 2, p. 941.
15 Ibid., pt 1, p. 30.
16 Ibid., p. 353.
17 *CTM*, no. 210, p. 542.
18 Ibid.
19 Gray, *Oaths*, p. 122.
20 *SL*, no. 54, p. 217.
21 Ibid., p. 220.
22 Ibid., p. 221.
23 Ibid., p. 222.
24 BL MS Cotton Manuscripts Cotton Cleopatra E/VI f.175v.
25 Roger Bigelow Merriman, *Life and Letters of Thomas Cromwell*, 2 vols [1968] (Oxford, 2000), vol. I, no. 71, p. 381.
26 *CTM*, no. 202, p. 508.
27 Ibid.
28 CW, vol. XII, p. 161.
29 *CTM*, no. 206, p. 515.
30 Ibid., p. 516.
31 Ibid., p. 524.
32 Ibid., p. 525.
33 CW, vol. XIV, pt 1, pp. 59, 239, 243.
34 Roper, *Life*, p. 44.
35 Lehmberg, *Reformation Parliament*, p. 203.
36 G. R. Elton, '1. The Law of Treason in the Early Reformation', *HJ*, XI/2 (1968), pp. 211–36 (p. 231).
37 MacCulloch, *Thomas Cromwell*, p. 267.
38 Translated in Louis L. Martz and Richard S. Sylvester, 'Thomas More's Prayer Book', *YULG*, XLIII/2 (1968), pp. 53–80 (p. 76).
39 Ibid.

40 The account is from CTM, no. 214, pp. 551–4.
41 Ibid., no. 216, pp. 555–6.
42 Henry Ansgar Kelly, Louis W. Karlin and Gerard B. Wegemer, eds, 'Appendix 1: Documents', in *Thomas More's Trial by Jury: A Procedural and Legal Review with a Collection of Documents* (Woodbridge, 2011), document 5, p. 145.
43 Ibid., document 10, p. 159.
44 Ibid.
45 Ibid., document 14, p. 171.

Epilogue

1 CW, vol. III, pt 2, no. 188, p. 221.
2 'For he shall give his angels charge over thee, to keep thee in all thy ways. They shall bear thee up in their hands, lest thou dash thy foot against a stone' (Psalms 91:11–12).
3 Cresacre More, *The Life of Sir Thomas More*, ed. Joseph Hunter (London, 1828), pp. 4–15.
4 John N. King, *Foxe's 'Book of Martyrs' and Early Modern Print Culture* (Cambridge, 2006), p. 113.
5 Thomas More, *Utopia*, ed. Joanne Paul (Oxford, 2025), p. 5.
6 John McGurk, *The Elizabethan Conquest of Ireland: The 1590s Crisis* (Manchester, 2009), p. 23.
7 'Utopian', adj., *Oxford English Dictionary*, 1.2.a.
8 Edward Hall, *Hall's Chronicle* (London, 1809), p. 817.
9 Anthony Munday and Others, *Sir Thomas More*, ed. Vittorio Gabrieli and Giorgio Melchiori (Manchester, 2009), 2.3.78–93 (pp. 100–101).
10 Ibid., 2.3.94–5 (p. 101).
11 Ibid., 5.4.49 (p. 202).
12 Ibid., 5.4.52–5 (p. 202).
13 Ibid., 5.4.71–2 (p. 204).
14 J. A. Sharpe, '"Last Dying Speeches": Religion, Ideology, and Public Execution in Seventeenth-Century England', *P. & P.*, 107 (1985), pp. 144–67.
15 Munday and Others, *More*, 5.4.114–8 (pp. 206–7).
16 *The Times*, 11 January 1935.
17 R. W. Chambers, *Thomas More* (London, 1935), p. 5.
18 Richard Marius, *Thomas More* (London, 1984), p. xx.
19 John Guy, *Thomas More: A Very Brief History* (London, 2000), p. xi.
20 Joanne Paul, *Thomas More: A Life* (London, 2025), p. 554.

21 David Daniell, *William Tyndale: A Biography* (New Haven, CT, 1994).
22 Guy, *Thomas More*, p. 88; Hilary Mantel, 'Letter to Thomas More, Knight' (Frick Collection, 2018), p. 5.
23 Kate Maltby, 'Like Isis, Thomas More Believed Passionately in Burning People Alive', *The Spectator*, 19 February 2015.
24 Mantel, 'Letter', p. 11.

BIBLIOGRAPHY

The standard edition of More's writings is *The Complete Works of St Thomas More*, ed. Louis L. Martz et al., 15 vols (New Haven , CT, 1962–97), which contains all the texts with extensive introductions and commentary. There is also *The Essential Works of Thomas More*, ed. Gerard B. Wegemer and Stephen W. Smith (New Haven, CT, 2020), which contains all the writings, with more limited notes and commentary, alongside an account of his trial. Its concision makes it an ideal entry-point for the non-specialist reader. The standard edition of the letters is *The Correspondence of Sir Thomas More*, ed. Elizabeth Frances Rogers (Princeton, NJ, 1947). There are many editions of *Utopia*, more recent than the Yale edition by Edward Surtz and J. H. Hexter (vol. IV, 1965), which provide helpful commentary and notes, including *Utopia*, ed. George M. Logan and Robert M. Adams, 3rd edn (Cambridge, 2016); ed. David Harris Sacks (New York, 1999); ed. and trans. George M. Logan, 3rd edn (New York, 2010), which includes a number of critical essays; and ed. Joanne Paul (Oxford, 2025), based on the sixteenth-century Robinson English translation. There is a useful edition edited by Richard S. Sylvester, *The History of King Richard III and Selections from the English and Latin Poems* (New Haven, CT, 1976), which is taken from the Yale edition.

The most recent biography is Joanne Paul, *Thomas More: A Life* (London, 2025), which situates More in the intellectual context of the Reformation, as well as detailing his family and political life at Henry VIII's court. Richard Marius, *Thomas More: A Biography* (New York, 1984), is still valuable – although it sometimes relies on dubious psychological assumptions – as is R. W. Chambers' pioneering *Thomas More* (London, 1935), which is factual but perhaps a bit too cautious and laudatory for contemporary readers. Peter Ackroyd's *The Life of Thomas More* (London, 1998) provides a good overview of More's life but is less strong on the works. John Guy, *The Public Career of Sir Thomas More* (New Haven, CT, 1977), outlines the significance of More's time in office; Guy, *A Daughter's Love: Thomas and Margaret More* (London, 2008), is an archive-based study for the general reader. Guy's *Thomas More* in the Reputations Series (London, 2000) provides useful reading alongside any of the above biographies. *Two Early Tudor Lives: The Life and Death of Cardinal Wolsey by George Cavendish and The Life of St Thomas More by William Roper*, ed. Richard S. Sylvester and Davis P. Harding (New Haven, CT, 1962), enables readers to compare and contrast these two accounts of the lives of two of the most significant figures of Henry VIII's reign. Also beneficial is Nicholas Harpsfield, *The Life and Death of Sir Thomas More*, ed. Elsie Vaughan Hitchcock (London, 1932), another biography by someone who, like Roper, knew More. Gerard B. Wegemer and Stephen W. Smith, eds, *A Thomas More Source Book* (Baltimore, MD, 2004), is a valuable collection of documents. J. B. Trapp and Hubertus Schulte Herbrüggen, *'The King's Good Servant': Sir Thomas More (1477/8–1535)* (London, 1977), a catalogue for an exhibition, contains relevant portraits, images and items relating to More's life and times.

General books on More include *The Cambridge Companion to Thomas More*, ed. George M. Logan (Cambridge, 2011), which is divided into three sections: life, times and work; five major works (*Utopia*, *The History of King Richard III*, the work on heresy and later consolation works); and More's afterlife. Joanne Paul, *Thomas More* (Cambridge, 2017) is a useful, succinct guide, as are John Guy, *Thomas More: A Very Brief History* (London, 2000), Anthony Kenny, *Thomas More* (Oxford, 1983), and Louis L. Martz, *Thomas More: The Search for the Inner Man* (New Haven, CT, 1990). Stephen Greenblatt's chapter, 'At the Table of the Great: More's Self-Fashioning and Self-Cancellation', in his *Renaissance Self-Fashioning: From More to Shakespeare* (Chicago, IL, 1980), pp. 11–73, is a stimulating analysis of the ways in which More thought about his life and significance. Travis Curtright's *The One Thomas More* (Washington, DC, 2012) offers a corrective to a tendency in the scholarship to create 'multiple Mores'. For a deep analysis of More's education and life choices see Gerard B. Wegemer, *Young Thomas More and the Arts of Liberty* (Cambridge, 2011) and Frank Mitjans, *Thomas More's Vocation* (Washington, DC, 2023). The journal *Moreana* (Edinburgh, 1963–) is devoted to the study of Thomas More.

On More and Erasmus see E. E. Reynolds, *Thomas More and Erasmus* (New York, 1965); Dominic Baker-Smith, 'Erasmus and More: A Friendship Revisited', *Recusant History*, XXX/1 (2010), pp. 7–25, which unpacks the complicated relationship between the humanist and religious elements of their relationship; and, on their friendship in terms of the European Republic of Letters and books possessed and exchanged, J. B. Trapp, *Erasmus, Colet and More: Early Tudor Humanists and Their Books* (London, 1991). It is also worth exploring the vast resource of *The Collected Works of Erasmus* (Toronto, 1975–).

Not surprisingly there are more works on *Utopia* than the rest of More's works put together. The recent guide, Cathy Shrank and Phil Withington, eds, *The Oxford Handbook of More's 'Utopia'* (Oxford, 2023), contains essays on almost every aspect a reader could want, from counsel and travel writing to a wide range of early modern and modern translations into languages including Latin, Spanish, French and Italian; from religion and architecture to philosophy and socialist interpretations. Important critical studies include J. H. Hexter, *More's 'Utopia': The Biography of an Idea* (Princeton, NJ, 1952), which was the first major study to outline the probable relationship between Books One and Two. Quentin Skinner, 'Thomas More's *Utopia* and the Virtue of True Nobility', in *Visions of Politics*, vol. II: *Renaissance Virtues* (Cambridge, 2002), pp. 213–44, situates the dialogue within the context of Renaissance neoclassical debates. Books on Utopianism and the influence of More's book in the sixteenth and seventeenth centuries include Robert Appelbaum, *Literature and Utopian Politics in Seventeenth-Century England* (Cambridge, 2002), which explores its impact on the civil war; Chloe Houston, *The Renaissance Utopia: Dialogue, Travel and the Ideal Society* (Aldershot, 2014), which explores the ways in which *Utopia* inspired authors to think of ideal societies from the reign of Henry VIII to the Restoration; and Terence Cave, ed., *Thomas More's 'Utopia' in Early Modern Europe: Paratexts and Contexts* (Manchester, 2008).

On More's humanism see Arthur Kinney, *Humanist Poetics: Thought, Rhetoric, and Fiction in Sixteenth-Century England* (Amherst, 1986), which explains why Lucian mattered so much to More and Erasmus. Anna Peterson, 'Dialoguing with a Satirist: The Translations of Lucian by Desiderius Erasmus and Thomas More', *International Journal of the Classical Tradition*, XXVII/2 (2020), pp. 71–92, shows how More's and Erasmus's versions of Lucian differed significantly. Paul Oskar Kristeller's article, 'Thomas More as a Renaissance Humanist', *Moreana*, XVII/65–6 (1980), pp. 5–22, remains a touchstone on the topic.

Alison Hanham provided a useful breakdown and comparison of the English and Latin versions of More's *History of King Richard III* in 'The Texts of Thomas More's *Richard III*', *Renaissance Studies*, XXI/1 (2007), pp. 62–84, and, in the same journal, Hans Yoran explored how the *History* might represent More's critique of his own humanist method: 'Thomas More's *Richard III*: Probing the Limits of Humanism', XV/4 (2001), pp. 514–37.

Valuable works on heresy and More's dispute with Tyndale include Eamon Duffy, '"The comen knowen multytude of crysten men": *A Dialogue Concerning Heresies* and the Defence of Christendom', in *The Cambridge Companion*, ed. Logan, pp. 191–215. Brian Cummings, 'Different Tongues:

More versus Tyndale', in *The Literary Culture of the Reformation: Grammar and Grace* (Oxford, 2002), pp. 190–96, part of a longer discussion of the Reformation and translation, is both insightful about literature and religion in More, as is Cummings' chapter, 'The Reformed Conscience: Thomas More', in *Mortal Thoughts: Religion, Secularity and Identity in Shakespeare and Early Modern Culture* (Oxford, 2013), pp. 67–91. Richard Rex, 'Thomas More and the Taking of William Tyndale', *Reformation*, XXVIII/2 (2023), pp. 134–43, argues that More had nothing to do with Tyndale's arrest and execution, despite popular myths that he did. A useful comprehensive account of More's religious polemics can be found in Brian Gogan, *The Common Corps of Christendom: Ecclesiological Themes in the Writings of Sir Thomas More* (Leiden, 1982). Mark Rankin's important re-evaluation, 'More's Confutation of Tyndale and its Readers', will be published in *Moreana* (2026).

Henry Ansgar Kelly, Louis W. Karlin and Gerard B. Wegemer, eds, *Thomas More's Trial by Jury: A Procedural and Legal Review with a Collection of Documents* (Woodbridge, 2011), gathers together and interprets the trial and execution of Thomas More; Andrew Hadfield, *Lying in Early Modern English Culture: From the Oath of Supremacy to the Oath of Allegiance* (Oxford, 2017), pp. 37–50, also provides an interpretation of the events.

Accounts of More's legacy often intertwine with studies of life writing. John Maquire, 'William Roper's *Life of More*: The Working Methods of a Tudor Biographer', *Moreana*, VI/23 (1969), pp. 59–65, established this association, and Warren Wooden, 'Structural Patterning in William Roper's *Life of More*', *Moreana*, XVI/64 (1980), pp. 100–106, connected his biography to medieval hagiographies. More recently, Alan Stewart has treated 'The Dangerous Lives of Sir Thomas More', in *The Oxford History of Life Writing*, vol. II: *Early Modern* (Oxford, 2018). A more tongue-in-cheek consideration of More's legacy comes from the author of *Wolf Hall*, Hilary Mantel, in her 'Letter to Thomas More, Knight' (Frick Collection, 2018), which forms the basis for a summary consideration of More's biographies and divided legacy by Joanne Paul in a Review Essay in *Studies in Medieval and Renaissance History*, XV (2018), pp. 313–23.

ACKNOWLEDGEMENTS

We are grateful to Michael Leaman, François Quiviger and an anonymous reader, all of whom commented on the text and made many useful suggestions, as well as saving us from a number of errors. Andrew Hadfield is grateful to Brian Cummings, who has been generous in sharing his immense knowledge of Erasmus. A number of papers at the 2025 SEDERI conference in Granada were helpful in his thinking about More. Joanne Paul would like to thank Quentin Skinner for fifteen years of support and guidance in thinking about Renaissance humanism.

Both authors are especially grateful to the little ones in their lives, who provided joyous interruptions during the writing of this book.

PHOTO ACKNOWLEDGEMENTS

The author and publishers wish to express their thanks to the sources listed below for illustrative material and/or permission to reproduce it. Some locations of artworks are also given below, in the interest of brevity:

Beinecke Rare Book and Manuscript Library, Yale University, New Haven, CT: pp. 164, 169; Biblioteca Nacional de España, Madrid: pp. 10–11; Bibliothèque nationale de France, Paris (MS NAF 28882, fol. 5v): p. 63; British Library, London (Cotton MS Titus D IV, fol. 12v): p. 20; Cambridge University Library: p. 156; The Frick Collection, New York: pp. 30, 37; Galleria Borghese, Rome: p. 129; Gallerie degli Uffizi, Florence: p. 45; Gleeson Library, University of San Francisco: p. 125; The Huntington Library, San Marino, CA: p. 54; John Carter Brown Library, Brown University, Providence, RI: p. 98; Kunstmuseum Basel: pp. 22, 32; The Metropolitan Museum of Art, New York: pp. 18, 27, 66; Museum Boijmans Van Beuningen, Rotterdam: p. 101; The National Gallery, London: pp. 71 (on loan from Longford Castle, Earl of Radnor Collection), 116; National Library of Australia, Canberra: p. 13; National Portrait Gallery, London: pp. 62, 161, 178; Rijksmuseum, Amsterdam: p. 132; © Royal Collection Enterprises Limited 2026 | Royal Collection Trust: pp. 14, 26, 29, 33, 58, 117; Universitätsbibliothek Basel: pp. 124, 126; Veste Coburg: p. 90; The Weiss Gallery, London: p. 23; Wikimedia Commons: pp. 184 (photo Mitrius, public domain), 185 (photo Giogo, CC BY-SA 4.0), 191 (photo Daderot, public domain).

INDEX

Page numbers in *italics* in refer to illustrations